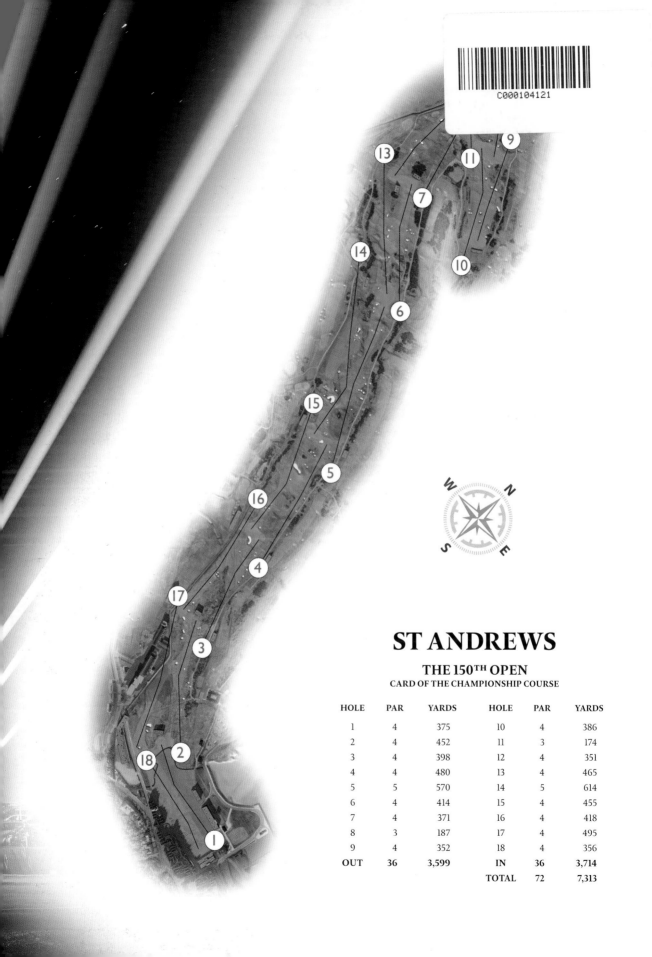

ST ANDREWS

THE 150TH OPEN
CARD OF THE CHAMPIONSHIP COURSE

HOLE	PAR	YARDS	HOLE	PAR	YARDS
1	4	375	10	4	386
2	4	452	11	3	174
3	4	398	12	4	351
4	4	480	13	4	465
5	5	570	14	5	614
6	4	414	15	4	455
7	4	371	16	4	418
8	3	187	17	4	495
9	4	352	18	4	356
OUT	36	3,599	IN	36	3,714
			TOTAL	72	7,313

Aurum Press
74-77 White Lion Street, London N1 9PF

Published 2022 by Aurum Press

Copyright 2022 R&A Championships Limited

Course illustration by Strokesaver

Project coordinator: Sarah Wooldridge
Additional thanks to:
Ed Hodge, Stuart Moffatt and Mike Woodcock at The R&A
SMT – SportsMEDIA Technology
Peter Kollmann
Rob Harborne

A CIP catalogue record for this book is available
from the British Library

ISBN 978-0-7112-8285-8

Designed and produced by TC Communications Ltd
Printed in Italy by L.E.G.O.

EDITOR
Andy Farrell

WRITERS AND PHOTOGRAPHERS

Writers	The R&A	Getty Images	R&A Photo Editors
Peter Dixon	Richard Heathcote	Andrew Redington	Kate McShane
Robert Green	Stuart Franklin	Ross Kinnaird	Cliff Hawkins
John Hopkins	Oisin Keniry	Warren Little	Alex Burstow
Lewine Mair	Tom Shaw	Harry How	
Art Spander	Charlie Crowhurst	Kevin Cox	
Alistair Tait	Stuart Kerr	David Cannon	
	Stephen Pond		
	Tom Dulat		

FOREWORD

By Cameron Smith

What a week it was! I can't quite believe it even now. To win an Open Championship is likely to be a highlight of any golfer's career. To do it around St Andrews, at The 150th Open, is unbelievable. In all my dreams, I had never dreamt as far as that. Yet here is the Claret Jug beside me to prove it happened.

St Andrews is such a cool place. I love the town and I love the golf course. Thanks to The R&A, the St Andrews Links Trust, the superintendents, the volunteers and everyone for making The 150th Open special. I thought the golf course was exactly as an Open Championship links should play, firm and fast. It was unreal.

Thanks to all my team — the hard work over the last couple of years has definitely been worth it. Unfortunately, my family were not with me at St Andrews. My dad was due to come over. He loves his golf and it would have been such a cool week at the home of golf. He was definitely kicking himself for not making it over, but that does not matter now. All the memories we've shared since, those memories will last a lifetime.

To all the fans at St Andrews, you were great. Especially, the Aussies! There seemed to be a lot of you, and your support kept me plugging away. To see my name on the Claret Jug alongside those of Peter Thomson and Kel Nagle at St Andrews, as well as Greg Norman and Ian Baker-Finch, means everything. As I said at the presentation, this one was for Oz.

THE R&A
OPEN CHAMPIONSHIPS
COMMITTEE

CHAIRMAN
David C Meacher

DEPUTY CHAIR
Áine Binchy

COMMITTEE
Alick Bisset
Tim Cockroft
Gavin Lawrie
Hans Lindeblad
Ada O'Sullivan
Alastair Wells

CHIEF EXECUTIVE
Martin Slumbers

EXECUTIVE DIRECTOR – CHAMPIONSHIPS
Johnnie Cole-Hamilton

EXECUTIVE DIRECTOR – GOVERNANCE
David Rickman

INTRODUCTION

By David C Meacher, Chairman, The R&A Open Championships Committee

Welcome to The 150th Open Annual, which celebrates the momentous staging of golf's original championship over the Old Course in St Andrews. Anticipation was high and it was wonderful to see a record 290,000 fans attend and enjoy a thrilling week of spectacular golf over a fast-running links in excellent condition.

The brilliant final round performance from Cameron Smith, especially on the back nine which included five birdies in a row, saw the Australian become Champion Golfer of the Year as he secured his first major title. It was a superb contest for the Claret Jug with Cameron Young's closing eagle earning him the runner-up spot and Rory McIlroy's gallant display seeing him finish third.

It was fitting for the home of golf to host the landmark anniversary of the Championship — the 30th time in total over the Old Course — with the unforgettable moments enjoyed by the fans in attendance and the millions watching across the world.

From our headquarters in St Andrews, everyone at The R&A relished the once-in-a-lifetime opportunity to celebrate this historic milestone. The 150th Open began with a very special four-hole exhibition of golf for fans young and old. The R&A Celebration of Champions comprised a distinguished field made up of past Champion Golfers, women's major winners, amateur champions and golfers with disability champions to highlight The R&A's commitment to inclusivity in the sport. It was a unique atmosphere and provided a fitting start to an exciting week shared by players and spectators alike. Experiencing The Open at St Andrews again proved something special and we were delighted to welcome HRH The Princess Royal. While the players had the chance to test their abilities over the famous links, fans could soak in the historic surroundings and savour the action in the ideal weather.

To present a Championship of such stature required a great deal of hard work from staff, contractors, local agencies and volunteers and my thanks go to everyone involved who contributed to the staging. I would also like to express my gratitude to St Andrews Links Trust, the local golf clubs and the town of St Andrews for their contribution to the Championship.

We hope you enjoy this annual to relive the memories of an historic week for The Open and for golf.

THE HOST OF GOLF

By Robert Green

The 150th staging of The Open took place over the Old Course at St Andrews this past July. The occasion had been deferred for 12 months because of the Covid pandemic but it proved to be no less notable for that. Far from the case, in fact, as Australia's Cameron Smith covered the back nine on Sunday in just 30 shots to claim victory by a stroke from Cameron Young. Golf can't get much more championship-calibre than that.

St Andrews has come to be regarded as the most fitting host of The Open on special anniversaries, such as the Centenary Open in 1960, the Millennium Open in 2000 and the 150th anniversary of its first playing in 2010. If any of the few people who might have claimed to be golf historians had been celebrating The Open after its 15th birthday, they would have wondered why on earth was anybody rabbiting on about St Andrews? The 15th Open, like the first dozen, had been played at Prestwick; St Andrews' sole claim to Championship fame had witnessed Tom Kidd's triumph of 1873. But Prestwick has not hosted The Open since 1925; this summer Smith became the 30th champion to prevail over the Old Course.

The final hole, where Smith drove to the edge of the green on the final day and then decisively got down in two putts, is known as "Tom Morris", named for the father of the father-and-son combination who won the title four times apiece between 1861-1872 (all at Prestwick, as it happened). The 10th is called "Bobby Jones" after the greatest amateur golfer in history, who won The Open there in 1927 and The Amateur Championship there in 1930, the year he completed the "Impregnable Quadrilateral", the original version of

what has evolved into the Grand Slam. Had Rory McIlroy ended the week victorious, rather than two shots adrift, the bunker shot he holed there for an eagle two on Saturday may have been the shot most remembered from this Championship.

Before the First World War, two British golfers, JH Taylor (1895 and 1900) and James Braid (1905 and 1910), won consecutive Championships at St Andrews. The third member of the "Great Triumvirate", Harry Vardon, who won a record six Opens, didn't win one of them over the Old Course. Since the Second World War, two American players have emulated Taylor and Braid: Jack Nicklaus (1970 and 1978) and Tiger Woods (2000 and 2005). That's pretty select company. Between Jack's last win and Tiger's first, we had victories by the two most stellar names in the history of European golf: Seve Ballesteros in 1984 and Sir Nick Faldo in 1990. (For the record, we also had John Daly in 1995, who remains in a category all of his own.)

St Andrews is the spiritual home of the game. The Royal and Ancient Golf Club of St Andrews was one of the game's two governing bodies until those duties, along with those of running The Open, passed to its modern offshoot, The R&A. The Old Course itself is likely the tract of land in Scotland over which golf has been played for longer than any other. The place has universally come to be recognised as the "home of golf". It was in 1552 that the public there were granted the right to "play at golf, football, schuting, at all gamis with all uther, as ever they pleis and in one time". That sentence may nowadays read like a word salad concocted by a delinquent predictive-text system, but the bigger picture would suggest that golf had in fact been played over that ground, if perhaps at times furtively, for a good while before 1552.

If a contemporary golf course architect handed his

Tiger Woods hits his tee shot at the hole named after Old Tom Morris.

prospective client the card of the course for the Old Course as part of his submission, I fear he would not get the commission. Only two par threes and two par fives. Those vast double greens, seven of them, leaving only four holes with individual greens. A short par four to begin and another to finish, sharing a joint fairway the size of an aircraft hangar and not a bunker in sight. No, the Old Course only works because it is the Old Course.

Not that the other 16 holes are bereft of sand. Some of the bunkers have suitably terrifying names — I offer you "Coffins", "Grave" and "Hell" — although the most notorious is surely "Road", on the par-four 17th. Bernard Darwin, the golf correspondent on *The Times* in the days when such correspondents went unnamed, described the bunker as "eating its way into the very vitals of the green". In 1970, Doug Sanders played an exquisite bunker shot here to save his par. It should have been the shot that won The Open. But he missed a short putt for par on the 18th and Nicklaus beat him in a play-off. No such drama occurred to Tommy Nakajima in 1978 or David Duval in 2000, but the fact that they both took four shots to extricate themselves from the sand on the Road Hole stands vivid testimony to the perils it can represent. And it is easy to overlook

what a fine examination of strategic golf the Old Course presents: drive to the left off the tee and you'll generally be safe, but left with a considerably more demanding second shot than if one had aimed to the right.

Bobby Jones' love affair with the "auld grey toun" was thoroughly reciprocated. In 1958, by then crippled with the spinal disease that had been tormenting his life for the previous 10 years, he returned as captain of the American Eisenhower Trophy team and was made a Freeman of the Burgh of St Andrews. He was only the second American to be so honoured. The first, in 1759, had been Benjamin Franklin, one of the Founding Fathers of the United States of America. Jones told his audience in the Younger Hall: "I could take out of my life everything except my experiences at St Andrews and I'd still have a rich, full life." The ovation he received left most attendees in tears. After his speech he clambered into his electric golf cart and was driven out of the building by Henry Longhurst, the BBC golf commentator.

Not everyone loves the Old Course, however, even those who have been successful on it. The 1946 winner, Sam Snead, seven times a major champion, commented that it "was so raggedy and beat up I was surprised to see what looked like fairway among the

Viktor Hovland plays from the huge Shell at the seventh. Strath is the pot bunker in front of the 11th green on the left.

The steep-faced bunkers of the Old Course remain a source of terror, as Kevin Na discovered in Hell on the 14th hole.

weeds. Down home we wouldn't plant cow beets on land like that". Of course, that may have been as much a reflection on the comparative poverty of immediately post-War Britain as anything else.

More recently, though, esteemed American golfing visitors have drawn more from the Jones playbook. Nicklaus said: "There isn't a place I would rather win a championship than on the Old Course at St Andrews." At the Masters Tournament in April, Woods, on returning to the fray for the first time since a near-fatal car crash in February 2021, said: "I am looking forward to St Andrews. That is something near and dear to my heart. It's the home of golf and it's my favourite course in the world, so I will be there for that one. Anything in between that, I don't know." He even skipped the US Open at Brookline, a very tough walking course, in order to be sure to make it. His emotional response to the tumultuous reception he received as he walked up

ST ANDREWS CHAMPIONS

Year	Champion	Year	Champion	Year	Champion
1873	Tom Kidd	1910	James Braid	1970	Jack Nicklaus
1876	Bob Martin	1921	Jock Hutchison	1978	Jack Nicklaus
1879	Jamie Anderson	1927	Bobby Jones[A]	1984	Seve Ballesteros
1882	Bob Ferguson	1933	Denny Shute	1990	Nick Faldo
1885	Bob Martin	1939	Dick Burton	1995	John Daly
1888	Jock Burns	1946	Sam Snead	2000	Tiger Woods
1891	Hugh Kirkaldy	1955	Peter Thomson	2005	Tiger Woods
1895	JH Taylor	1957	Bobby Locke	2010	Louis Oosthuizen
1900	JH Taylor	1960	Kel Nagle	2015	Zach Johnson
1905	James Braid	1964	Tony Lema	2022	Cameron Smith

The spiritual home of golf: St Andrews provided a setting both ancient and modern for The 150th Open.

The Bear honoured by St Andrews

Jack Nicklaus quoted from Bobby Jones when he received honorary citizenship of St Andrews, as Jones and Benjamin Franklin had before him. Nicklaus was feted at a ceremony in Younger Hall that included the awarding of honorary degrees from the University of St Andrews to Sir Bob Charles, Sandy Lyle, Catriona Matthew, Jose Maria Olazabal and Lee Trevino in recognition of their achievements and outstanding service to the game of golf. Nicklaus, golf's Golden Bear, received the same honour in 1984.

"The people of St Andrews were unbelievable," Nicklaus said of his second win on the Old Course in 1978. "They welcomed us with open arms, hanging from the rooftops as we finished. I'll never forget that reception I received. It was unbelievable.

"I returned in 1984 and I was bestowed an honorary doctor of law degree from the University of St Andrews, a wonderful honour. You humbled me then just as you are humbling me today.

"It remains one of my proudest moments as a golfer and a person. There seemed to be a mutual admiration and love affair between the people of Scotland, St Andrews and me.

"All the experiences I had at St Andrews, and I was here on eight occasions to play The Open, have been something I will love and cherish forever — and so will my family. Thank you so much for this wonderful honour. To quote Bobby Jones, 'I could take out of my life everything except my experiences at St Andrews and I'd still have a rich, full life'. I feel exactly the same.

"I'm now 82 years old, 44 years removed from my last win. As Grantland Rice wrote they rarely remember as quickly as they forget so let me say thank you for remembering and not forgetting me and, most importantly, thank you for allowing me to be what I always felt I was for so many decades — one of you. Thank you, St Andrews."

the final fairway on Friday, missing the cut by some margin, spoke volumes as to his affection for the place.

After his victory in 2022, Smith echoed similarly appreciative sentiments. "To win an Open Championship in itself is probably going to be a golfer's highlight in their career. To do it in St Andrews, I think is just unbelievable. This place is so cool. I love the golf course. I love the town."

Two days before the on-course action got seriously underway, Nicklaus had joined Franklin and Jones in being made an honorary citizen of St Andrews. He had not returned to the town since his farewell wave from the Swilcan Bridge at The Open in 2005 but, he said, "when I got the invitation ... to follow Bobby

Jones and Benjamin Franklin, I've got to come back". The following day, there was a memorial service in that same Younger Hall to remember and celebrate the life of Peter Alliss, the legendary BBC commentator, widely hailed as the "Voice of Golf", who died in December 2020 at the age of 89. There was an added poignancy, too. In 1978, at the prize-giving just before Nicklaus was presented with the Claret Jug, there had been warm words from The R&A for Henry Longhurst, Alliss' predecessor at the BBC, Jones' chauffeur 20 years beforehand, whose illness had prevented him from carrying out his customary commentating duties. Longhurst passed away within the week.

The Old Course, however, is essentially immortal,

despite the odd bits of course lengthening and tee rearranging. After all, one suspects there were a few dark mutterings about the town in the mid 1760s when it was decided that, in the wake of William St Clair having covered the course's 22 holes in a mere 121 strokes, it would be redesigned to be 18 holes — which eventually led to that becoming the norm everywhere else as well. There is limited scope for increasing the yardage at St Andrews and yet the Old Course still found a way to test the latest generation of the game's best players and provide four days of compelling theatre.

As ever, it had hosted a championship that was all about the golf. To a substantial degree, the same could be said of the town.

St Andrews is all about the golf.

New Zealand's Ben Campbell attempting to unlock the secrets of the immortal Old Course in a practice round.

A celebration for the whole game

Peter Dixon on the Champions showcasing all that is good in golf

As a 10-year-old child growing up in Holywood, Northern Ireland, Rory McIlroy undertook a school project on his sporting hero. There are no prizes for guessing that the chosen subject was a golfer by the name of Tiger Woods.

Fast forward 23 years to the home of golf and McIlroy was to be seen as part of an acclaimed fourball that was made up of Woods himself, Lee Trevino and Georgia Hall, major champions all.

The occasion was The R&A Celebration of Champions on the Monday of The 150th Open at St Andrews — four holes played in a better ball format — and the four of them were in illustrious company. In total there were 10 teams made up of Champion Golfers, women's major champions, male and female amateur champions and golfers with disability champions, including Kipp Popert, who became the first golfer with disability to play in The Amateur Championship at Royal Lytham & St Annes a month earlier.

"If you'd told 10-year-old Rory back then that he'd be doing this he wouldn't have believed you," McIlroy said. "It's quite emotional. To be as close as I am with my hero growing up, to be doing this with Tiger, Lee Trevino, Georgia Hall, all the great champions that are gathered here today ... it's a pinch yourself moment. I'm privileged and humbled to be a part of it all."

In warm and dry conditions, the crowds gathered to see legends of the game at close quarters, those still active and challenging for the highest honours, as well as those whose best days are behind them but who will be forever feted as some of the finest players to have graced the Royal and Ancient game.

It would be fair to say that the Woods' fourball attracted more than its share of attention. There were plenty of smiles and laughter — Trevino, at 82, showed that he is still the course jester he always was ("I can't wait to get up in the morning just to hear what I have to say") — and one never-to-be-forgotten moment when the four were joined by Jack Nicklaus, arguably the greatest champion of them all, for a photograph on the Swilcan Bridge.

For England's Hall, this was as good as it gets. Soon after, she was posting the photograph on social media with the words: "What dreams are made of." She had also made a lasting impression on McIlroy, who pronounced himself "super impressed".

Champions forever: Tiger Woods, Rory McIlroy, Jack Nicklaus, Lee Trevino and Georgia Hall pose for an historic picture.

THE OPEN QUALIFYING SERIES

❶ SOUTH AFRICA
Joburg Open
25-27 November 2021
Thriston Lawrence, South Africa
Zander Lombard, South Africa
Ashley Chesters, England

❷ SINGAPORE
SMBC Singapore Open
20-23 January
Sadom Kaewkanjana, Thailand
Yuto Katsuragawa, Japan
Joohyung Kim, Korea
Sihwan Kim, USA

❸ AUSTRALIA
Vic Open
10-13 February
Dimitrios Papadatos, Australia
Ben Campbell, New Zealand
Matthew Griffin, Australia

❹ JAPAN
Mizuno Open
26-29 May
Scott Vincent, Zimbabwe
Anthony Quayle, Australia
Brad Kennedy, Australia
Justin De Los Santos, Philippines

❺ CANADA
RBC Canadian Open
9-12 June
Keith Mitchell, USA
Wyndham Clark, USA

❻ KOREA
Kolon Korea Open
23-26 June
Minkyu Kim, Korea
Mingyu Cho, Korea

❼ NETHERLANDS, IRELAND AND SCOTLAND
Dutch Open
26-29 May
Victor Perez, France
Ryan Fox, New Zealand
Adrian Meronk, Poland

Horizon Irish Open
30 June-3 July
John Catlin, USA
Fabrizio Zanotti, Paraguay
David Law, Scotland

Genesis Scottish Open
7-10 July
Kurt Kitayama, USA
Jamie Donaldson, Wales
Brandon Wu, USA

❽ USA
Arnold Palmer Invitational
3-6 March
Chris Kirk, USA
Talor Gooch, USA

John Deere Classic
30 June-3 July
JT Poston, USA
Christiaan Bezuidenhout, South Africa
Emiliano Grillo, Argentina

Barbasol Championship
7-10 July
Trey Mullinax, USA

FINAL QUALIFYING

FAIRMONT ST ANDREWS
28 June
David Carey, Republic of Ireland
Robert Dinwiddie, England
Lars Van Meijel, Netherlands
Alex Wrigley, England

HOLLINWELL
28 June
Barclay Brown[A], England
Richard Mansell, England
Oliver Farr, Wales
Marco Penge, England

PRINCE'S
28 June
Matt Ford, England
Jamie Rutherford, England
Ronan Mullarney, Republic of Ireland
Jack Floydd, England

ST ANNES OLD LINKS
28 June
Marcus Armitage, England
Sam Bairstow[A], England
Matthew Jordan, England
John Parry, England

EXEMPT COMPETITORS

Abraham Ancer, Mexico — 4, 5, 12
Adri Arnaus, Spain — 7
Alexander Björk, Sweden — 5
Richard Bland, England — 5
Keegan Bradley, USA — 4
Dean Burmester, South Africa — 5
Sam Burns, USA — 4, 12
Mark Calcavecchia, USA — 1
Laurie Canter, England — 5
Patrick Cantlay, USA — 4, 12, 15
Paul Casey, England — 4, 5, 15
Filippo Celli[A], Italy — 25
Stewart Cink, USA — 1, 12
Darren Clarke, Northern Ireland — 1, 2
Corey Conners, Canada — 4, 12
John Daly, USA — 1
Bryson DeChambeau, USA — 4, 8, 12, 15
Thomas Detry, Belgium — 5
Stephen Dodd, Wales — 22
David Duval, USA — 1
Ernie Els, South Africa — 1, 2
Harris English, USA — 4, 12, 15
Jorge Fernández Valdés, Argentina — 14
Tony Finau, USA — 4, 12, 15
Matt Fitzpatrick, England — 4, 5, 8, 15
Tommy Fleetwood, England — 4, 5, 15
Dylan Frittelli, South Africa — 3
Sergio Garcia, Spain — 9, 12, 15
Justin Harding, South Africa — 5
Brian Harman, USA — 13
Padraig Harrington, Republic of Ireland — 1
Tyrrell Hatton, England — 4, 5, 6, 15
Russell Henley, USA — 4
Lucas Herbert, Australia — 4, 5
Kazuki Higa, Japan — 21
Garrick Higgo, South Africa — 5
Tom Hoge, USA — 4

Nicolai Højgaard, Denmark — 5
Max Homa, USA — 4
Billy Horschel, USA — 4, 5, 6, 12
Sam Horsfield, England — 7
Rikuya Hoshino, Japan — 4
Viktor Hovland, Norway — 4, 5, 12, 15
Mackenzie Hughes, Canada — 3
Sungjae Im, Korea — 4, 12
Shugo Imahira, Japan — 19
Aaron Jarvis[A], Cayman Islands — 28
Dustin Johnson, USA — 3, 4, 9, 12, 15
Zach Johnson, USA — 1, 2
Takumi Kanaya, Japan — 20
Chan Kim, USA — 20
Si Woo Kim, Korea — 4
Kevin Kisner, USA — 4
Brooks Koepka, USA — 3, 4, 8, 10, 12, 15
Jason Kokrak, USA — 4, 12
Pablo Larrazabal, Spain — 7
Paul Lawrie, Scotland — 1
Kyoung-Hoon Lee, Korea — 4
Min Woo Lee, Australia — 5
Marc Leishman, Australia — 4
Haotong Li, China — 7
Luke List, USA — 4
Shane Lowry, Republic of Ireland — 1, 2, 4, 5, 15
Robert MacIntyre, Scotland — 3, 5
Hideki Matsuyama, Japan — 4, 9, 12
Rory McIlroy, Northern Ireland — 1, 2, 4, 5, 11, 12, 15
Phil Mickelson, USA — 1, 2, 10
Guido Migliozzi, Italy — 5
Francesco Molinari, Italy — 1, 2, 6
Jediah Morgan, Australia — 16
Collin Morikawa, USA — 1, 2, 3, 4, 5, 10, 12, 15
Sebastián Muñoz, Colombia — 4

Kevin Na, USA — 4, 12
Keita Nakajima[A], Japan — 26, 27
Joaquin Niemann, Chile — 4, 12
Shaun Norris, South Africa — 17, 18
Louis Oosthuizen, South Africa — 1, 3, 4, 12
Mito Pereira, Chile — 4
Thomas Pieters, Belgium — 4, 5
Aldrich Potgieter[A], South Africa — 23
Ian Poulter, England — 5, 15
Seamus Power, Republic of Ireland
Jon Rahm, Spain — 3, 4, 5, 8, 12, 15
Aaron Rai, England
Patrick Reed, USA — 4, 9, 15
Xander Schauffele, USA — 4, 12, 15
Scottie Scheffler, USA — 3, 4, 9, 12, 15
Adam Scott, Australia — 4
Jason Scrivener, Australia — 5
Webb Simpson, USA
Cameron Smith, Australia — 4, 11, 12
Jordan Smith, England
Jordan Spieth, USA — 1, 2, 3, 4, 12, 15
Henrik Stenson, Sweden — 1, 2
Sepp Straka, Austria
Sahith Theegala, USA
Justin Thomas, USA — 4, 10, 11, 12, 15
Cameron Tringale, USA
Harold Varner III, USA
Lee Westwood, England — 15
Bernd Wiesberger, Austria — 5, 15
Danny Willett, England — 5, 6
Aaron Wise, USA
Gary Woodland, USA — 8
Tiger Woods, USA — 1, 9
Cameron Young, USA
Will Zalatoris, USA — 4, 5

KEY TO EXEMPTIONS FOR THE 150TH OPEN

Exemptions for 2022 were granted to the following:

(1) The Open Champions aged 60 or under on 17 July 2022
(2) The Open Champions for 2011-2021
(3) First 10 and anyone tying for 10th place in the 2021 Open at Royal St George's
(4) First 50 players on the OWGR for Week 21, 2022, with additional players and reserves drawn from the highest ranked non-exempt players in the OWGR as of June 30
(5) First 30 in the final 2021 DP World Tour rankings
(6) BMW PGA Championship winners for 2018-2021
(7) First five DP World Tour members and any DP World Tour members tying for fifth place, not otherwise exempt, in the top 20 of the Race to Dubai rankings on completion of the 2022 BMW International Open
(8) US Open Champions for 2017-2022
(9) The Masters Tournament Champions for 2017-2022
(10) The PGA Champions for 2016-2022
(11) The Players Champions for 2019-2022
(12) Top 30 players from the final 2021 FedEx Cup Points List
(13) First five PGA Tour members and any PGA Tour members tying for fifth place, not exempt in the top 20 of the PGA Tour FedEx Cup Points List for 2022 on completion of the 2022 Travelers
(14) 2021 VISA Open de Argentina Champion
(15) Playing members of the 2021 Ryder Cup teams
(16) First and anyone tying for first place on the Order of Merit o the Tour of Australasia for 2021-22
(17) First and anyone tying for first place on the Order of Merit o the Sunshine Tour for 2021-22
(18) Japan Open Champion for 2021
(19) Asia-Pacific Diamond Cup Champion for 2022
(20) First two and anyone tying for second place, on the Official Money List of the Japan Golf Tour for 2021
(21) First and anyone tying for first place, not exempt in a cumulative money list taken from all official 2022 Japan Gol Tour events up to and including the 2022 Japan Tour Championship
(22) Senior Open Champion for 2021
(23) Amateur Champion for 2022
(24) US Amateur Champion for 2021
(25) European Amateur Champion for 2022
(26) Mark H McCormack Medal winner for 2021
(27) Asia-Pacific Amateur Champion for 2021
(28) Latin America Amateur Champion for 2022

YOUNG AT HEART OF THE 150ᵀᴴ

By Andy Farrell

Rory McIlroy called it golf's Holy Grail. "It does feel like the biggest Open we've ever had," said Tiger Woods. Any Open Championship at St Andrews is special. "It's history every time we get a chance to play here," Woods added. For the 30th time, the Old Course was hosting and appropriately, too, for The 150th Open. It really was more historic, more special.

And certainly bigger, in terms of record prize money and a record attendance, with 290,000 fans attending for the week. Nothing quite like it had been seen before. Was a week ever so eagerly anticipated? By Woods even more so, the picture of returning to the hallowed ground foremost in his mind while recuperating from his devastating car crash in 2021. And by everyone simply for having endured a pandemic that had seen this occasion postponed by a year.

Of the previous milestone championships celebrated in St Andrews, including the Centenary Open in 1960, and the 150th anniversary Open in 2010, it was perhaps the Millennium Open in 2000, with Woods at the peak of his powers, that came closest to capturing the sense of both excitement and expectancy. That was the week with the previous biggest attendance of 239,000. More now were making the pilgrimage, and despite the travails of air, rail and road transportation.

So it was a sweet moment, at 6.35 on Thursday morning and after The R&A Celebration of Champions, the ceremonies and festivities, the dinners and reunions, when Paul Lawrie struck the opening tee shot. "I was surprised how many people were here," he said. "I wasn't expecting that." The Champion Golfer from Carnoustie in 1999 was out of his usual routine.

"I normally like watching the game ahead tee off. I've always got to the tee really early my whole career. I couldn't do that this morning, there was no one there. But I put a nice swing on it and popped it down the fairway. No bother."

Lawrie had received a call from Martin Slumbers, Chief Executive of The R&A, prior to the Championship. "Mr Slumbers phoned me a couple of weeks ago and asked if I'd do it," Lawrie said. "The first thing you think of is 'how cool is that?', being asked to do it. So it was lovely."

Also lovely was Lawrie's tee shot at the 18th when he returned to that unique amphitheatre of ancient buildings and modern grandstands. On turf almost as straw-coloured as his yellow ball, his drive scampered along the rolling fairway, diving into and out of the Valley of Sin, and cresting onto the green where it finished five feet from the hole. One of the shots of the day. An eagle to finish. Was there the odd member's bounce in there? It would only be right since Lawrie, along with Woods and McIlroy, had just been announced as honorary members of The Royal and Ancient Golf Club of St Andrews.

More pertinently, it illustrated the fast-running nature of the links and the fact that the morning starters were to have the best of the seaside conditions, with wind picking up throughout the day. Among those to get out early were amateur Barclay Brown with a 68, Cameron Smith with a 67, his namesake Cameron Young with a 64 and then McIlroy with a 66. A number of 68s and 69s followed, but the only other score of five under par or better came in the penultimate game of the day, a 67 from Robert Dinwiddie.

A stunning debut in The Open for Cameron Young with a 64.

Bucket list day for amateur Brown

If Barclay Brown had been looking for inspiration on his first appearance at The Open, he needed to look no further than Matt Fitzpatrick, a fellow member of the Hallamshire Golf Club in Sheffield who also happened to be the reigning US Open champion.

One of six players from the unpaid ranks in the field, Brown came through qualifying at Hollinwell. A Walker Cup player, Brown was distinctive in his camouflage bucket hat. It was the quality of his play, however, that most caught the eye. Out at 6.45am with the second group of the day, the 21-year-old Stanford University student set the early pace with a four-under-par round of 68, highlighted by a birdie at the 17th. At the end of the day's play he was joint fifth, four strokes behind America's Cameron Young.

"I was unbelievably nervous at the start," he said. "Then once I got through the first couple of holes it was nice to calm down a little and hit some good shots. I had a good chat with Sir Nick Faldo and Darren Clarke before coming out and they were able to help. They said keep it out of the bunkers and get good at hitting 60-foot putts."

And the early tee time? "When I saw the draw I said, 'it's not too bad because I'll probably be awake at 4am anyway. I might as well be out playing golf rather than sitting twiddling my thumbs'."

Brown had joined an English national team practice the week before at Royal St George's, venue for the previous year's Open. It proved to be good preparation for mixing it with the pros on the Old Course. "I think amateurs are comfortable with it," he said. "So many of the big events that we play as UK players, it's links golf all year round."

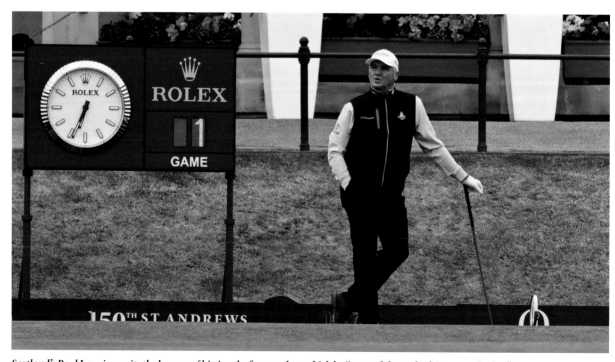

Scotland's Paul Lawrie awaits the honour of hitting the first tee shot, which he "popped down the fairway, no bother".

An unfortunate start for Tiger Woods, whose second shot at the opening hole found the burn leading to a double bogey.

It was quite a debut in The Open for Young, a 25-year-old American who came close to winning the PGA Championship in May. For 12 holes he made more birdies than pars and then he made a three at the last for his 64, eight under par. But it was not his first time on the Old Course. As a 13-year-old in 2010, Young played with his father and he attracted attention for using the back tees. "My dad had to get permission," Young explained. "I'm glad I didn't know or I would have been nervous out of my mind. When we came out to hit our first tee shots with the R&A building right there, there were a bunch of R&A members watching.

"There's just no hiding how special this place is," Young added. "And it's certainly been a goal to get to an Open Championship. And for my first one to be here is a little bit extra special for me."

It was not a perfect round, he accepted, but he had thought his way around well. He had a couple of extra days to prepare after missing the cut at the Genesis Scottish Open the previous week, a performance he put down to jet lag. Not that he was an instant expert, he realised. "I don't think I've figured that much of it out, honestly," Young said. "You could play every day here for a year and you would just scratch the surface of what you can know about this place. There's so many humps, and little nuances to the golf course, that we could never know in the four or five days that I've

had to prepare. So a lot of it is accepting that, and figuring out as much as we can. I think we probably have seen about five per cent of what's out there. There's a pretty endless amount to take in."

A long putt from almost 30 feet at the second green helped, followed by a 10-footer for a second birdie at the third. He was on the par-five fifth in two and made his four, then hit a wedge at the sixth to seven feet to get to four under par. He drove over the green at the ninth, chipped back and tapped in for a three. He was leading The Open and no one matched his outward half of 31 all day. However, the moment of the day on the ninth had come from Ian Poulter, when the Englishman holed a putt from around 162 feet across the entire width of the green for an eagle-two. No wonder Poulter peered at the ball disappearing as if sighting a ship on the horizon. Another Englishman never managed to tee up, Justin Rose withdrawing in the morning due to a back injury, while Erik van Rooyen also had to default at the last minute.

Young, in a rookie season on the PGA Tour that had included a number of second and third places, was already one of the longest hitters on the circuit. He has a pause at the top of the backswing that suggests a man gathering himself, checking everything is in order, before going ahead and giving the ball an almighty thwack. He also drove through the green at the 12th,

Padraig Harrington down on one knee to line up a putt on the first green.

EXCERPTS FROM THE PRESS

"From the moment he arrived in this ancient seaside village earlier this week, Rory McIlroy has had a confident bounce in his step, a cloak of calmness enveloping him."

—Steve DiMeglio,
USA Today

"It was McIlroy's return to his fast-starting self that allowed the 60,000-strong galleries to take a positive storyline into the Fife night."

—James Corrigan,
The Daily Telegraph

"The first time Cameron Young played the Old Course at St Andrews was one of his best moments in golf: The most recent one was even better."

—Doug Ferguson,
Associated Press

"The galleries were six, seven, even eight or nine deep. What they saw was not vintage Woods, though. Far from it. But if Woods has lost some of his threat, he has lost none of his appeal."

—Moira Gordon,
The Scotsman

"The crowds never deserted him, not even when it was dinner time and Tiger was still on the course. They carried on cheering whenever his golf allowed it, and they cheered him all the way up the 18th."

—Owen Slot,
The Times

A good start for Rory McIlroy as he finished the day two behind the leader.

Cameron Smith, with a nautical air, sailed around the Old Course in 67.

which is one way of taking all the trouble out of play. Again he chipped back close for his birdie, having already made a two at the 11th with a two-footer.

The background of a new young player can take time to unravel, but one interviewer who noted Young attended a school in the Bronx reputed for producing basketball players and that it was "an improbable journey from the streets of New York" was a little wide of the mark. "I think the 'streets of New York' is probably a stretch," Young deadpanned. "I took the train to school, but I also took the train back home to go practise." Young grew up at Sleepy Hollow Country Club in Westchester, where his dad, David, is the head professional. His mum played golf, his aunt is also a professional. "It might sound a little improbable, but I've been around golf my whole life," added the Wake Forest graduate.

At the par-five 14th, he had a long eagle putt to get to nine under with four to play. But he three-putted and then had to wait until the 18th for his eighth birdie of the day. The other 10 holes he parred. He had hit all 18 greens, large though they may be, in regulation. At that point he was leading by three strokes from Smith.

It was an unobtrusive beginning for the Australian, although on a chilly morning he was wearing a natty nautical jacket that made it look like he had just arrived at the local marina, in contrast to Justin Thomas, whose joggers made it appear as if he had just arrived from the gym. It didn't take this noted putting maestro long to get the speed of the greens. Smith rolled in a 55-footer at the second to get his campaign under way. He got up and down from a bunker at the fifth for a four and was four under after 10 before his only bogey of the day at the 11th. He then birdied the 12th and got what was rapidly becoming a regulation three at the 18th to post his 67.

"Always nice to get off to a good start in the majors," said Smith, who played a practice round alongside Marc Leishman and Adam Scott that was watched by tennis player Ashleigh Barty, a fellow Queenslander who won the Australian Open in January 2022, to add to her 2021 Wimbledon crown, and promptly retired. This was Smith's fifth Open appearance but his first at the Old Course, although he had played in the St Andrews Links Trophy as an amateur. "Places like this almost give you goosebumps," he said. "Standing on the first tee at St Andrews in an Open is something that I've only dreamed about as a kid."

Smith added: "It was probably some of the best lag putting I've ever done. My putt on the second managed to go in from a fair distance, that was pretty decent, but I seemed to have so many 80, 90,

Two-time winner Ernie Els was going well until a double bogey at the 17th hole.

IT'S A
FACT

Cameron Young became the 11th player to score 64 or better in the first round of The Open. No one has yet gone on to win. Rory McIlroy at St Andrews in 2010 and Phil Mickelson at Royal Troon in 2016 each scored 63s. Louis Oosthuizen, who holds the record lowest opening score by a Champion Golfer of 65 in 2010, also scored 64 at Royal St George's in 2021 without winning.

Young delivering another almighty thwack as the American drives at the fourth tee.

EXCERPTS FROM THE PRESS

"The epochal shift presaged a decade ago when Rory McIlroy was re-shaping the post-Tiger Woods era with four majors by the age of 25 has been slow to materialise. Perhaps it needed the tides of history to converge on this monumental setting to finally come to pass."

—Kevin Garside,
i newspaper

"It continued a positive trend of fast starts at the majors for McIlroy, who previously opened 65 at the PGA Championship in May and 67 at the US Open in June."

—Adam Schupak,
Golfweek

"Bob MacIntyre admits he suffered a severe St Andrews sweat when his last-hole birdie came with beads of perspiration still dripping from his forehead. He diced with danger as he skirted the out of bounds up the right."

—Craig Swan,
Daily Record

"DeChambeau could overthink the timing of a boiled egg, but what madness there is in his method has served him well: stiff-armed, robotic, resolutely single plane right down to his putting, and all of it married to a searing golfing intelligence."

—Kevin Mitchell,
The Guardian

"Day one of The 150th Open did not disappoint. Of course it didn't, because it never disappoints. It had a little bit of everything."

—Mark Cannizzaro,
New York Post

McIlroy led the way within one of the featured groups of the opening round.

A relaxed Justin Thomas contemplates a putt during an opening 72.

100-footers out there today and I did a good job of getting down in two."

Among those on 68, one behind Smith, were world number one Scottie Scheffler and Viktor Hovland, who had to take a penalty drop for an unplayable lie in a bunker at the 12th, but was the only player in the field to birdie the last three holes. Ernie Els, on the 10th and 20th anniversaries of his two Open triumphs, might have joined them until the South African drove into the hotel at the 17th.

The Road Hole, however, was not at its most fearsome, not even the hardest hole on the course, which was the 13th — where playing away from the pin was advisable for the second shot in order to have a chance to get close in three — followed by the fourth. Moment of the day at the 17th was Si Woo Kim leaving his third shot in the Road Hole bunker, only to hole the next one for his par.

McIlroy, for strange reasons, was playing in only his second Open at St Andrews. He missed 2015, when he was supposed to be the defending Champion, due to an injury sustained playing football. In 2010, the young Northern Irishman had been the first-round leader with a 63. Then came an 80 the next day. It had been a long time to wait for redemption. An opening 66 here meant he had still not scored in the 70s in an Open at St Andrews.

He opened nicely, holing a 55-footer on the first green back towards the cup that was cut just over the burn. But he really started motoring from the fifth with three birdies in a row. Three more at 12, 14 and 18, with a bogey at 13, added up to six under, two behind Young. "Fantastic start," he said. "Just what you hope will happen starting off your week. I did everything that you're supposed to do around St Andrews. I birdied the holes that are birdieable. And I made pars at the holes where you're sort of looking to make a par and move to the next tee. And didn't really put myself out of position too much."

McIlroy added: "It's another good start at a major. Three in a row for me now. And looking forward to the next few days." Before the PGA in May, and the US Open in June, McIlroy had been on a bad run of falling behind out of the gate in majors. Just think of the disastrous opening to The Open in his homeland in 2019. But confidence had steadily been growing in his

Firm foundations for Dinwiddie

Qualifier Robert Dinwiddie spends part of his time working in a friend's construction company. A golf career that stalled due to back issues following Walker Cup honours and three Challenge Tour victories may not have turned out as the Scottish-born resident of Wandsworth, south London expected, but his third appearance in The Open, and second at St Andrews, was built on firm foundations with an opening 67.

Playing in the penultimate game of the day, and finishing after 10pm, the 39-year-old Dinwiddie made five birdies prior to his only bogey of the round at the 16th, then made a three on the 18th green. "It was a fantastic day to be able to put together a good score," he said. "I was playing well. I just try to give every shot 100 per cent with concentration, effort and commitment. You expect it to be a long round and I had plenty of food in my bag. It is a test physically, mentally and it is dark and getting cold. It was tough."

A 77 the next day meant Dinwiddie went on to make the cut for the first time at The Open, and he closed with a 69 to tie for 53rd place and earn $35,656. No more kitchens to be fitted for a while, he returned to the Challenge Tour with renewed confidence. "My aim was to enjoy the whole week, and then after making the cut, that allowed me to do that even more. I enjoyed all of it, hit some good shots, and even managed to get it out of the Road Hole bunker there on 17. So all in all, I'm really chuffed."

Young drove to the edge of the 18th green and two-putted for his eighth birdie of the round.

game. A drive of over 380 yards at the 14th left him with just a wedge for his approach shot. But that drive had leaked into the rough on the left and he caught a flier with the second and finished over the green, getting up and down for birdie to make amends for the bogey at the previous hole.

"This is the fiddliest Open that I've played," McIlroy said. "It's the only way I can describe it. And fiddly hasn't really been my forte over the years, but I'm hopefully going to make it my forte this week."

Ironically, someone who hit an even longer drive at the 14th was Woods, who had the longest of the day at 412.3 yards. He even made one of only three birdies he achieved all day. It had all gone wrong, after the long

wait for his 2.59pm tee-time, at the first. No member's bounce for Woods. His tee shot finished in a divot, his second in the burn, and he missed a short putt, ending up with a six. He went out in 41. Still the crowd remained to see the three-time Champion Golfer home at the end of a long six-hour round, but it added up to a score of 78.

"This was always on the calendar to hopefully be well enough to play," Woods said. "And I am. I just didn't do a very good job of it."

There was still time for Dinwiddie to do a great job in matching Smith's 67 as night fell on a Young-at-heart sort of day. Every day at The Open at St Andrews is that sort of day.

Round of the Day: Cameron Young - 64

OFFICIAL SCORECARD
THE 150TH OPEN
ST ANDREWS

Cameron YOUNG
Game 11
Thursday 14 July at 8.25 am

FOR R&A USE ONLY (1.1)

THIS ROUND 54

ROUND 1
18 HOLE TOTAL

64

VERIFIED NW

ROUND 1

Hole	1	2	3	4	5	6	7	8	9	Out	10	11	12	13	14	15	16	17	18	In	Total
Yards	375	452	398	480	570	414	371	187	352	3599	386	174	351	465	614	455	418	495	356	3714	7313
Par	4	4	4	4	5	4	4	3	4	36	4	3	4	4	5	4	4	4	4	36	72
Score	4	3	3	4	4	3	4	3	3	31	4	2	3	4	5	4	4	4	3	33	64

Signature
of Marker

Signature of
Player
Cameron Young

Si Woo Kim pops out from the Road Hole bunker as his second attempt goes in for a par.

66 *I think there's very few places where length really wouldn't play to your advantage. I'm going to have one less bunker in play than some other people.* 99
—Cameron Young

66 *I need to go out tomorrow and back up what I just did today. I think that's important to do.* 99
—Rory McIlroy

66 *I'm watching Peaky Blinders at the moment. I'll probably watch five or six episodes this afternoon.* 99
—Cameron Smith

66 *I hit it two cups out to the right on nine. Look, anything inside six feet from 160 feet is a helluva putt. So for it to drop is beyond lucky.* 99
—Ian Poulter

66 *Just that one shot on 17 is going to keep me burning until tomorrow.* 99
—Ernie Els

66 *I kid you not, I think the fairways are faster than the greens in some spots. They are? I'm glad I'm not losing my mind.* 99
—Scottie Scheffler

66 *It was a dream-come-true type day, minus some of the golf. It really felt like fantasy to play with Tiger.*99
—Max Homa

66 *I've never had any more 70, 80, 90-foot putts in my life. They put the pins in good spots. Those were Sunday pins.*99
—John Daly

66 *Today was a blur. Hit some good drives and hit a bad second, hit some good second shots and hit a bad putt. Never got any momentum going.* 99
—Collin Morikawa

Americans Xander Schauffele and Collin Morikawa in conversation during their opening rounds.

After almost going out of bounds, Ian Poulter plays his second shot at the first from beside the Swilcan Burn on the 18th.

FIRST ROUND LEADERS

HOLE	1	2	3	4	5	6	7	8	9	OUT	10	11	12	13	14	15	16	17	18	IN	TOTAL
PAR	4	4	4	4	5	4	4	3	4	36	4	3	4	4	5	4	4	4	4	36	72
Cameron Young	4	3	3	4	4	3	4	3	3	31	4	2	3	4	5	4	4	4	3	33	64
Rory McIlroy	3	4	4	4	4	3	3	3	4	32	4	3	3	5	4	4	4	4	3	34	66
Cameron Smith	4	3	4	4	4	4	3	3	4	33	3	4	3	4	5	4	4	4	3	34	67
Robert Dinwiddie	3	4	4	4	3	4	3	4	4	33	3	3	4	4	5	3	5	4	3	34	67
Barclay Brown(A)	4	4	4	4	5	4	3	3	3	34	5	3	3	4	4	4	4	3	4	34	68
Kurt Kitayama	4	4	4	4	4	4	2	4	4	34	4	3	3	4	4	4	4	4	4	34	68
Lee Westwood	4	6	4	3	4	4	3	3	3	35	3	3	4	4	4	3	4	5	3	33	68
Brad Kennedy	3	4	3	4	4	4	3	4	5	34	3	2	5	5	4	4	4	4	3	34	68
Viktor Hovland	3	4	3	5	5	4	4	3	3	34	4	3	4	5	5	4	3	3	3	34	68
Talor Gooch	3	3	4	4	4	4	5	4	3	34	4	3	3	4	6	4	4	3	3	34	68
Dustin Johnson	3	4	4	5	5	4	4	3	3	35	4	2	3	4	4	5	4	4	3	33	68
Scottie Scheffler	4	4	3	3	4	4	4	3	3	32	4	3	4	5	4	4	4	4	4	36	68

■ EAGLE OR BETTER   ■ BIRDIES   □ PAR   ■ OVER PAR

SCORING SUMMARY

FIRST ROUND SCORES

Players Under Par	54
Players At Par	22
Players Over Par	80

Low First Nine

Cameron Young	31

Low Second Nine

Wyndham Clark	33
Russell Henley	33
Dustin Johnson	33
Si Woo Kim	33
Joaquin Niemann	33
John Parry	33
Adam Scott	33
Lee Westwood	33
Cameron Young	33

LOW SCORES

Low Round

Cameron Young	64

FIRST ROUND HOLE SUMMARY

HOLE	PAR	YARDS	EAGLES	BIRDIES	PARS	BOGEYS	D.BOGEYS	OTHER	RANK	AVERAGE
1	4	375	0	29	106	17	4	0	12	3.974
2	4	452	0	13	101	34	7	1	5	4.244
3	4	398	0	28	105	17	6	0	10	4.006
4	4	480	0	10	75	65	6	0	2	4.429
5	5	570	3	52	82	15	4	0	14	4.776
6	4	414	0	20	101	32	3	0	9	4.115
7	4	371	0	25	109	21	1	0	11	3.987
8	3	187	0	13	110	33	0	0	8	3.128
9	4	352	2	70	73	10	0	1	17	3.609
OUT	36	3,599	5	260	862	244	31	2		36.269
10	4	386	0	29	109	18	0	0	13	3.929
11	3	174	0	7	99	46	3	1	4	3.308
12	4	351	2	70	59	17	6	2	15	3.750
13	4	465	0	2	84	58	12	0	1	4.513
14	5	614	3	59	74	18	2	0	16	4.724
15	4	455	0	12	107	37	0	0	7	4.160
16	4	418	0	13	106	32	4	1	6	4.192
17	4	495	0	11	85	50	8	2	3	4.391
18	4	356	2	82	70	2	0	0	18	3.462
IN	36	3,714	7	285	793	278	35	6		36.429
TOTAL	72	7,313	12	545	1,655	522	66	8		72.699

Winners abound at this Open of all Opens

Lewine Mair discovers the lengths some players went to in order to tee it up at St Andrews

You did not have to be Cameron Smith to feel like a winner at The 150th Open. There were spectators for whom finding a room in St Andrews was good reason to celebrate, while there were overseas visitors who were cock-a-hoop at touching down in Scotland with their luggage intact. And then, of course, there were those players who arrived at the Championship at the 11th hour, either via Open Qualifying or, rather more precariously, the reserve list.

Among the players, the most arresting of late-in-the-day fairytales belonged to England's Aaron Rai. On the Wednesday afternoon, The R&A rang Rai at his home in Wolverhampton. After delivering the news that he had moved up from third alternate to second, they wanted to know if he was prepared to come up to St Andrews on the off-chance of getting into the field. "Aaron did his packing and he was off," said his father, Amrik. "He's usually the reverse of a last-minute guy but he was desperate to play in such a very special Open."

Aaron and his caddie, Jason Timmis, drove up in Timmis's camper van and, on arriving in St Andrews at an hour when the town was too silent to start ringing on guesthouse doorbells, they stayed put in the vehicle.

In the meantime, things were stirring anew on that reserve list.

Justin Rose, who had been having through-the-night treatment for the lower back injury he had sustained in his Wednesday practice round, pulled out of the Championship ahead of his 8.14am starting time and his place was taken by Japan's Rikuya Hoshino. Next, South Africa's Erik van Rooyen, whose back was playing up, followed suit. His place went to Rai, who, having had no more than four hours sleep, had the phone call of his dreams at 10am. He would be teeing off at 1.48pm.

When Rai handed in an opening 75, he was not about to make excuses. As far as he was concerned, "It was just great to be out there."

Like Rai's experience, Trey Mullinax's journey to St Andrews was as exhausting as it was exhilarating. On the preceding Sunday, he had been playing in the Barbasol Championship on the PGA Tour, the

Japan's Rikuya Hoshino made his second appearance in The Open after Justin Rose withdrew on Thursday morning.

Aaron Rai drove to Scotland in his caddie's van on Wednesday and played at St Andrews on Thursday as the last player into the field.

Kentucky event which served as the last qualifying opportunity for The Open.

With none of the field down to play at St Andrews, there were no two ways about it. Only the winner would have the chance of heading for Scotland.

So little did the 30-year-old Mullinax fancy his chances — he had never won on the PGA Tour — that he had not bothered to pack his passport. The psychologists may or may not think that was a good move but, either way, the player ended up slotting a nerveless 15-footer which served as the first leg of his 5,000-mile journey to St Andrews. "What an honour to be able to play there," he cried. "I'm super-excited to have the chance to figure out that course!"

Following a southbound flight to his home in Alabama to pick up his passport and his father, Chip, a well-known actor, the pair took off for New York — and from there to Dublin before a fourth and final flight to Edinburgh.

There was one more hazard to negotiate. Once at R&A HQ, Mullinax (left) unzipped his golf travel-case to discover some of his clubs had ended up badly bent.

Mullinax may have had "none to zero sleep" but, instead of a weary sigh, he insisted that he felt thrice blessed that they had arrived at all.

The equipment people, who were busier than they had ever been with such issues, sorted him out and, finally, he was underway. "That was such fun," he said after a practice round with Jordan Spieth. It looked it. Furthermore, Mullinax's first round 71 did nothing to spoil a story with which he and Chip will no doubt be regaling friends and family for years to come.

For another father-son pilgrimage to St Andrews, what of Marcus Armitage and his father, Philip? When, two weeks earlier, Marcus had shared the top Final Qualifying spot at St Annes Old Links with Sam Bairstow, he and Philip set about arranging a trip to St Andrews which went to the very heart of their golfing beings.

To explain, Armitage's mother, Jean, had died when Marcus was 14 and when, in 2021, he won the Porsche European Open, this much-loved golfer spoke of how he had dreamed of such a result every night since his mother's death.

On the Tuesday at St Andrews, he and his father shared a quiet moment on the links, a moment in which they thought of Jean, of how she had paved the way for Marcus's success and how much she would have cherished the thought of father and son coming to this Open of Opens together.

SMITH PUTTS HIMSELF IN CONTENTION

By Andy Farrell

Mid-afternoon on Friday at The 150th Open. There was something in the air. St Andrews golf aficionados could smell it. The wind was switching. Out at the loop, new leader Cameron Smith had driven the 10th green. Back at the 18th hole, the green was not so easily in range off the tee. But the grandstands were packed. Every vantage point occupied. Tissues, it turned out, needed to be within range. That other thing in the air was tears.

Friday on the 18th of the Old Course is not about winning ancient goblets. It is about farewells and thanks for coming. Might be big or small. That walk still means something whether you are Mark Calcavecchia, given the honour of teeing off first in the second round to mark the 1989 Champion Golfer's final appearance, or qualifier Alex Wrigley, a teaching professional from Hartlepool in his first Open with, as caddie, new bride Johanna Gustavsson, the Ladies European Tour player who herself would be teeing up in the AIG Women's Open at Muirfield the following month.

For Tiger Woods, it felt like a full Old Course salute. Would he stop on the Swilcan Bridge? No. This was not the full Palmer-Nicklaus farewell. But the cap came off and, as he continued his march up the most famous fairway in golf, it only went back on out of necessity. His eyes were watering. The ovation kept going and going. There was an impromptu nature to it. If this was the last time ... Only then did it seem to hit the great man. Until then he had been consumed with getting here, recuperating his crushed body, competing for the Claret Jug again, even if it meant missing the cut. Suddenly, amid the affection, the

thought of how many more St Andrews might there be for him? This might be the last time. Depending on when The Open returns to the home of golf, depending on that fragile body, depending on whether he could remain a golfer at all, competitive or ceremonial.

On the ovation went. There were nods of respect from friends such as Rory McIlroy, walking down the first fairway, and Justin Thomas, still on the first tee. "It was a cool moment to be on that fairway when that was happening," McIlroy said. "Everyone hopes it's not the end of his Old Course career. I think he deserves, we deserve, him to have another crack at it."

Only time will tell. At that precise moment McIlroy had other things to worry about. "Like the wind switch I got on the wedge shot," he said. "Then that 60-footer back towards the burn, and you're thinking it wouldn't really look good if you putted one into the water." He did not hole as the previous day, but it was a par to start. By this point of the second round, however, McIlroy, who overnight was lying second, two behind Cameron Young, had been pushed down the leaderboard.

There was already a lot to catch up on. Heavy overnight rain, which lingered as showers through the first part of the morning play, had greened up the course from the previous day. "It was still firm," said Dustin Johnson, "but it was definitely a lot softer."

Johnson knows his way around the Old Course. "It was a really solid day, hit a lot of quality iron shots, never really got out of position," he said after a 67. He holed from almost 30 feet at the 16th to tie Young at eight under par, then two-putted the 18th to set the early clubhouse lead at nine under. At 135, the two-

---

Cameron Smith leapt to the top of the leaderboard with a 64.

EXCERPTS FROM THE PRESS

"It was clear by late on the first nine that Woods would have difficulty making the cut. He put a lot of effort into making it back for The 150th Open and succeeded. His game just did not cooperate."

—Bob Harig,
Sports Illustrated

"All week, Smith has swept around the Old Course with the smoothest swing in Fife. He has reached a state of grace to which few players can aspire, holding a pose after every approach and putting so impeccably that the ball seemed to be on rails."

—Oliver Brown,
Daily Telegraph

"As they exchanged understanding glances and walked in opposite directions on parallel paths — Woods on the 18th hole, McIlroy on the first — it felt like a passing of the torch."

—Christopher Clarey,
The New York Times

"To think, no player called Cameron has ever won a major. Now, after waiting more than 160 years, two men clearly capable of becoming the first have come along at once."

—Derek Lawrenson,
Daily Mail

"Strap yourself in because The 150th Open is shaping up to deliver something special over the final two days at St Andrews."

—Martin Dempster,
The Scotsman

A second successive 68 for Scottie Scheffler and a 66 for Tyrrell Hatton.

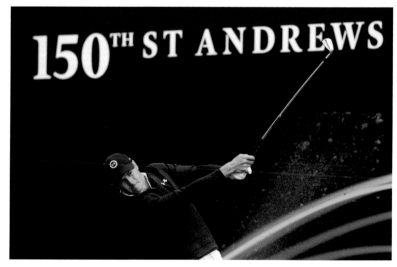

Jordan Spieth hits his tee shot at the eighth hole on his way to a 69.

Adam Scott (65) and Dustin Johnson (67) coped with the early morning rain to return impressive scores on Friday.

time major winner was a stroke behind where he was in 2015, when he led for the first two days only for a pair of 75s on the weekend to scupper his chances of being low "Johnson" as namesake Zach became Champion Golfer of the Year. "To be honest, I don't remember the third round from seven years ago," came the quintessential DJ response when asked about it. "That was a long time ago."

There was a 68 from world number one Scottie Scheffler, who matched only Johnson and Sahith Theegala in hitting all 18 greens in regulation, to get to eight under par, and Tyrrell Hatton, who missed the cut on his two previous St Andrews appearances in The Open, was on the same mark after a 66. Adam Scott, a day before his 42nd birthday, went one better with a 65 thanks to seven birdies and no bogeys, to get to seven under. Out at the loop, American Kurt Kitayama, a late qualifier at the Genesis Scottish Open, enjoyed himself with back-to-back twos. He birdied the eighth from eight feet and eagled the 352-yard ninth by hitting his drive to two feet. The Old Course can still confound, however, even when in less benign mode as China's Haotong Li discovered at the first. His second shot rebounded from the wall of the burn all the way back down the fairway, and then he put his third into the water.

Robert Dinwiddie, whose 67 on Thursday night when scoring was at its toughest for the week, one of the unsung achievements of The 150th Open, just made the cut on level par with a second round of 77. Overall, the late-early side of the draw still came out worse, with the later starters on Friday swarming to the top of the leaderboard. Chief among them was Smith, who took over as low "Cameron" by equalling Young's 64 from the first round.

It was to be one of the great putting rounds ever seen at the home of golf, or anywhere else. A player has done amazingly well to tally more than 100 feet of holed-putts in a round. Smith's total for Friday was an astonishing 253 feet. It mounted quickly as he holed from 47 feet at the first, 17 feet at the second and a mere 12 feet at the third. He hit a beautifully controlled wedge shot to six feet at the seventh, and then took the lead at 10 under par by making a near 30-footer at the eighth.

With the wind switching, the ninth was now playing against and he made a par, but the 10th was downwind and Smith hit a 396-yard drive onto the back of the green and two-putted for his birdie. Even when he was not holing everything he looked at, his lag putting was just as effective as the previous day. Yet then came the stunning moment of the par-five 14th, where he

Smith drives at the par-five 14th hole, watched by Brooks Koepka and Seamus Power.

covered the 600 yards to the front of the green in two blows, the second just creeping up the bank onto the main part of the putting surface. And then holed a monster 64-foot putt, curling from right to left at the end. The eagle took the Australian to 13 under par and three ahead.

"Once it started breaking pretty good, about 10-15 foot out, I thought it would have a chance," Smith said. "It was not really one you're trying to hole, you're just trying to get a nice easy birdie. But it was nice of it to pop in the side there."

Put Smith firmly in the camp of being a "feel" player when it comes to the long putts. "I'm basically just looking at the hole and trying to see the ball just dropping in the front there," he explained. "That's always been the last thought of mine, taking a long, hard, look at the hole and really feeling the putt. I don't take a practice stroke. I just get up there and really feel it."

He parred home for the 64, the lowest second round in a St Andrews Open, and, at 13 under par, set a record for 36 holes at any Open for a score under regulation figures. His total of 131 was also the lowest ever on the Old Course, one better than Sir Nick Faldo and Greg Norman in 1990, and Louis Oosthuizen in 2010. "Obviously, I got off to a really hot start," Smith said. "I stayed patient and hit some really nice putts. We probably played 16 holes into the wind today. We were able to land some of the approach shots into the green a little bit softer than the guys in the morning, but the tee shots were a little harder."

The 28-year-old Queenslander had won the Sentry Tournament of Champions at the start of the year, and then his biggest title to date, The Players Championship, in March. His form had dipped a little since but a strong showing in the Genesis Scottish Open the previous week had given Smith a "bit more of a pep in my step". Playing on firm and fast-running courses is second nature to the Australian, who had plenty of experience of playing on the great Sandbelt courses near Melbourne. "You have to play smart golf. You have to play away from the pin, use the slopes to your advantage. Sometimes, having a big curling putt is your best option. I think the Aussies will do good this week as it gets firmer and faster." Which he expected over the weekend. "Being late off again

IT'S A FACT

Cameron Smith's score of 13 under par set a new Championship record for most strokes under par after two rounds. The previous low mark was 12 under par set by Sir Nick Faldo and Greg Norman at St Andrews in 1990, then equalled by Faldo in 1992 at Muirfield, Tiger Woods in 2006 at Royal Liverpool, Louis Oosthuizen at St Andrews in 2010 and Rory McIlroy in 2014 at Royal Liverpool. Smith's two-round total of 131 was a record for the 36-hole score in an Open at St Andrews.

Kurt Kitayama plays from the road at the 17th hole, as Phil Mickelson observes.

Exciting times for Theegala

Cameron Young was not the only American rookie impressing at St Andrews. Sahith Theegala scored a 68 in the second round, following an opening 69, to make the cut for the first time in a major championship. The 24-year-old from California had twice qualified for the US Open.

A fan favourite already in the States, Theegala was eagerly cheered on at St Andrews, especially when holing from 50 feet for an eagle at the ninth.

A multiple award winner in college golf, he had enjoyed two high finishes in his first season on the PGA Tour, at the WM Phoenix Open and then the Travelers Championship. The latter performance, when he was runner-up to Xander Schauffele, helped Theegala rise up the world rankings and put him in position for a reserve spot in The 150th Open when Daniel Berger withdrew the previous week.

"I was very excited because of the magnitude of the event, not only my first Open, but St Andrews and The 150th," he said. "It took me a couple of days to settle down. I was walking the course on Monday and not really paying attention. Once I got to Tuesday, the normal prep started. It's been a blast the last two days, so much fun. Major championship golf is insane. To be here is doubly insane."

Theegala recalled his only previous experience of Scottish links golf was at Carnoustie — "the hardest course I've ever played" — a decade earlier. But growing up on public courses in California helped. "There's no water or grass, it's like hitting off hard pan. You learn to hit these spinning wedge shots. It's a little purer out here, obviously, but I think that definitely helped."

Collin Morikawa hits his second at the ninth. Having said it "sucked" to hand back the Claret Jug, he missed the cut.

Tiger Woods strides across the Swilcan Bridge.

With a 68 on Friday, Adrian Meronk made the cut after becoming the first player from Poland to play in The Open.

tomorrow afternoon, it's obviously going to be a bit firmer. I would say it's going to be pretty brutal out there."

At day's end, Smith led by two strokes from first-round leader Young. The New Yorker finished at 11 under par after a 69, with five birdies and his first two bogeys of the week. "Mostly good, I can't complain," Young said. "I didn't putt as well today, but for the most part I managed pretty well." There was not much for him to work on with his dad, the Sleepy Hollow professional and his coach. "Not much. Just really trying to keep things simple. Played it on the ground for the most part. Seems to be the best way to go around here."

One stroke further back were McIlroy and Viktor Hovland. Remarkably, of the 18 former Champion Golfers who teed up, McIlroy was one of only four to make the cut, which fell at level par, along with Jordan Spieth, Shane Lowry and Francesco Molinari. Woods was joined on the sidelines by the other St Andrews winners Zach Johnson, Oosthuizen and John Daly. Collin Morikawa, Henrik Stenson and Ernie Els all missed by one shot, Morikawa joining Darren Clarke and Ben Curtis as winners at Royal St George's who then missed the cut as defending Champions. Morikawa had said it "sucked" to give back the

Claret Jug at the start of the week, and the description of his putting over the two days was probably even more colourful.

On the other hand, four of the six amateurs competing qualified for the weekend race for the Silver Medal, the highest number since the last St Andrews Open in 2015. Barclay Brown still led the way after a 70 to be six under par, while Italy's Filippo Celli scored a 67 to be three under. Sam Bairstow, who came through Final Qualifying, and Aaron Jarvis, the first player from the Cayman Islands to play in The Open, also made it through. As did the first player from Poland to compete at The Open, Adrian Meronk, who followed an opening 75 with a 68.

Norway's Hovland lit up the evening play by holing his second shot for an eagle at the 15th from the wispy rough on the left of the fairway. "All that I was trying to do was finish 30 feet left of the pin and take my par," Hovland said. "As soon as I hit it, the ball drifted a little further right than I thought. I was a little concerned it was going to go too far right but it straightened out and somehow landed softly on that side slope and trickled in. That was unbelievable."

He also birdied the 18th for a 66 to share third place with McIlroy at 10 under par. The Northern Irishman started the second round slowly, but picked up shots

Smith decorated his scorecard with six birdies and an eagle at the 14th.

EXCERPTS FROM THE **PRESS**

Viktor Hovland smiles after his eagle at the 15th, where he did not need to putt.

"With Smith setting a brisk pace, those on the late shift tried their best to cling to his coat tails. You could say it was a charge of the fading light brigade."

—Kate Rowan,
The Daily Telegraph

"Rory McIlroy went from reducing Tiger Woods to tears to soaking up the St Andrews cheers on his charge towards Open glory."

—Jeremy Cross,
Daily Star

"Cam Smith is poised to shrug off the mantle as Best Player Yet To Win A Major. And do it on one of the most historic of golfing stages."

—Steve Scott,
The Courier

"Woods was as candid as he was regretful about his ordinary showing. Time and again, he could not push his hips convincingly through the shot, looking an almost timid shadow of the frightening athlete he once was."

—Kevin Mitchell,
The Guardian

"Were there ever galleries like it for a guy lying 148th? Was there ever such adulation for so bang ordinary a round? Surely not. But then again, there surely never was a star as magnetic as Tiger Woods."

—Bill Leckie,
The Sun

Emotional farewell for Calcavecchia

At the age of 62, Mark Calcavecchia did not expect to be playing in The 150th Open. The exemption for former Champions falls at 60 and yet the winner from Royal Troon in 1989 received a special extension to play at St Andrews and subsequently revelled in every minute of it.

With the Championship cancelled in 2020 because of the pandemic, and with back surgery putting paid to any chance of competing a year later, the American felt his Open career was already over. But he received an email from Martin Slumbers, Chief Executive of The R&A, offering him a place in the 156-man field and he could not have been more delighted.

Calcavecchia, who admitted to getting a "little choked up", was able to share the St Andrews experience with those closest to him – his wife, Brenda, who acted as caddie, his son, daughter and son-in-law. It was a true family occasion. While he did not make the cut with rounds of 83 and 82, he did get the chance to wave goodbye from the Swilcan Bridge in what was his 100th round in the Championship. As swansongs go, they do not get much better.

"I'm not sure what I was expecting, but I felt it. I felt the emotions," Calcavecchia said. "Forget about my golf. It wouldn't have mattered if I shot a pair of 75s or a pair of 85s, which I nearly did. It was about playing one more, my last one here at the home of golf.

"The fans were great," he added. "They were cheering for me and pulling for me and they were aware that this was my last Open. That was pretty cool. It means a lot. It really does."

at the fifth and the seventh before dropping one at the eighth.

His round started to gain momentum at the start of the back nine with three successive birdies. But at the 15th he drove into somewhat thicker rough than Hovland and he could not control the second shot. It ran to the back of the green, leaving a huge expanse between his ball and the hole that took three putts to negotiate.

Not dropping another shot at the 16th was an important moment in the round, and then he hit an approach to 23 feet at the 17th and holed for a birdie. Here was some good old, late night McIlroy drama and the gallery in the grandstand roared their appreciation. Another three at the 18th would have been the perfect nightcap but his tiny putt stayed out. A 68 it was.

"I would have taken playing the last two at one under, I just did it in the reverse of what I was thinking, three-four instead of four-three," McIlroy, three off the lead, said.

Tiger fans of all stripes and none lined the 18th fairway.

"I know I've got the game. That's all I need," he added. "If Cam Smith goes out and shoots another two rounds like he did the first two days, I'm going to have a hard time to win the tournament. So I've just got to do the best I can do and worry about myself, and hopefully it's good enough."

Open debutant Joohyung Kim on the 18th hole, where the 20-year-old Korean made a birdie for a 71.

Woods holds back the tears as he walks up the 18th fairway.

John Daly failed to qualify after three bogeys to finish.

Defending Champion Collin Morikawa.

> **"** I'm hitting a lot of great shots. I think you've just got to be aware that links golf is not fair. **"**
> —Viktor Hovland

> **"** Nice to be here for the weekend. My previous two Opens here, we were obviously going home early. **"**
> —Tyrrell Hatton

> **"** Yeah, I haven't tried haggis yet. You are correct. **"**
> —Scottie Scheffler

> **"** It's been brilliant. I've never played a tournament of this magnitude before. So to hear everyone shouting my name, it's pretty surreal. **"**
> —David Law

> **"** That double green hasn't been good to me this week. I'm four over. A double on the second yesterday and a double on 16 today. **"**
> —Shane Lowry

> **"** A ball is just running until something stops it, usually the rough or sand. If the wind was blowing 20 to 30, I don't know how you'd play this. **"**
> —Stewart Cink

> **"** It's pretty cool to have the challenge of the tough pins being close to some crazy slopes. If you are a little short, it comes back. If you are a little long, it runs away. Fun challenge. **"**
> —Corey Conners

> **"** On 15, I had a putt of 39 paces all up the hill into the wind. You can't practise this anywhere else in the world. **"**
> —Jon Rahm

Round of the Day: Cameron Smith - 64

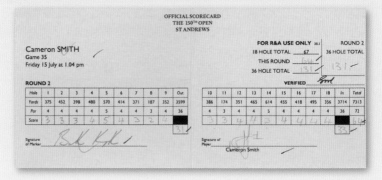

Cameron Young scored another sub-70 round to lie second to Smith by two strokes.

SECOND ROUND LEADERS

HOLE	1	2	3	4	5	6	7	8	9	OUT	10	11	12	13	14	15	16	17	18	IN	TOTAL
PAR	4	4	4	4	5	4	4	3	4	36	4	3	4	4	5	4	4	4	4	36	72
Cameron Smith	3	3	3	4	5	4	3	2	4	31	3	3	4	4	3	4	4	4	4	33	64-131
Cameron Young	4	5	4	3	4	4	4	3	3	34	4	3	4	4	4	5	4	4	3	35	69-133
Rory McIlroy	4	4	4	4	4	4	3	4	4	35	3	2	3	4	5	5	4	3	4	33	68-134
Viktor Hovland	4	4	4	3	4	4	3	3	4	33	3	4	4	5	4	2	4	4	3	33	66-134
Dustin Johnson	5	4	3	4	5	4	4	3	3	35	3	3	4	4	4	4	3	4	3	32	67-135
Scottie Scheffler	5	4	4	4	5	4	3	3	4	36	3	2	3	4	5	4	4	4	3	32	68-136
Tyrrell Hatton	4	4	4	4	5	3	3	3	3	33	3	3	4	4	4	4	4	4	3	33	66-136
Talor Gooch	3	4	4	4	5	4	4	3	4	34	4	3	4	4	4	4	5	4	3	35	69-137
Adam Scott	4	4	3	4	4	4	4	3	3	33	3	2	4	4	4	4	4	4	3	32	65-137
Patrick Cantlay	4	3	3	4	4	4	3	3	3	31	4	3	4	4	4	4	4	5	4	36	67-137
Sahith Theegala	5	4	3	4	4	4	4	4	2	34	4	3	3	4	4	4	4	4	4	34	68-137

Tears of the Tiger

Art Spander witnesses an emotional ovation for the two-time winner on the Old Course

the US Open at The Country Club, saving himself for a run in The 150th Open, but he shot 78 in the first round and 75 in the second.

From the very start, Woods was unfortunate. On Thursday, his tee shot on one finished in a divot, he dumped his approach shot into the burn and took a double-bogey six. From that point he never could recover. His championship was compressed to the starting and closing holes.

The other two golfers in the group, Homa and Fitzpatrick, the Englishman who triumphed at Brookline, seemed thrilled to be alongside Woods for those Thursday and Friday rounds. "It was amazing," said Fitzpatrick. "It gave me goosebumps. Just looking round and seeing the way everyone stood up. Giving him an ovation down 18. It was incredible. It is something that will live with me forever.

"It's thoroughly deserved, and I think towards the end you could see he was a little bit emotional as well. It was a big deal."

Fitzpatrick and Homa stayed back some as they walked the closing fairways, a fine compliment to a golfer they have admired for years. There was precedent. "I've seen it with other players who have done it up here before," said Fitzpatrick. "Max chided me a little bit, 'It's like you're a little bit close.' I'm like, panicking. Was I? 'No, we're all good'."

Woods insisted he is not leaving golf. "I'm not retiring from the game," he said. "It's a struggle just playing the three events I played this year. That in itself was something I'm very proud of. I was able to play these three events, considering what has transpired.

"Maybe something next year," he added. "It's hard just to walk and play 18 holes. People have no idea what I have to go through and the hours of work on the body, pre and post, each and every single day to do what I just did."

The Open in 2023 is at Royal Liverpool, Hoylake, where Tiger famously won in 2006, only once hitting his driver. Is it too much to ask if he will be up to the challenge?

He certainly met the challenge for The 150th Open. His presence, a special gift to the game.

Every vantage point was taken around the 18th hole as St Andrews saluted Woods at the conclusion of his second round.

ROARING FOR RORY IN A DUEL TO REMEMBER

By Andy Farrell

Any walk out to the loop of the Old Course, next to the Eden Estuary, is worth it. The setting is beautiful and, except perhaps in a howling gale, peacefully serene. And except for Saturday afternoon of The 150th Open. Thousands flocked to the far end of the course and it was the place to be in the third round. The atmosphere in the grandstands surrounding the greens and in the mini spectator village was tumultuous. Building up the infrastructure here to complement the town end of the course was a roaring success.

And there was no doubt who they were roaring for. "The support I've got this week has been absolutely incredible," said Rory McIlroy. "I appreciate it and feel it out there. The galleries have been massive."

The roars for Rors reached a crescendo at the 10th green, out in the cauldron of the loop, when McIlroy holed a bunker shot for an eagle and his name went to the top of the leaderboard for the first time.

"What a wild two on that hole," said Viktor Hovland, McIlroy's playing partner, who needed to hole his birdie putt immediately afterwards to retain a share of the lead. "I was glad I was able to make mine for birdie. But when things like that happen, you have to give each other a fist bump and say, 'good shot'."

Hovland played an equal part in a dramatic third round which ended with the two European Ryder Cup players tied for the lead. They had set out in the penultimate game of the day, each three behind the halfway leader Cameron Smith. The two Camerons in the final pairing, including New York's Young who started two behind the Australian, never matched their heroics of the first two days when each scored a 64. They could not keep up with the pair just in front

Saturday 66s apiece for Rory McIlroy and Viktor Hovland.

of them on the course and finished tied for third, four strokes behind, Smith after a 73 and Young with a 71.

McIlroy and Hovland both scored 66s to finish at 16 under par. Smith and Young were at 12 under, Masters champion Scottie Scheffler (69) and Si Woo Kim (67) a stroke further back and Dustin Johnson was at 10 under par after a 71.

But it was the pairing of McIlroy and Hovland that captured the attention. Hovland went ahead by holing a succession of long putts on the way to four birdies in a row. McIlroy kept in touch, three birdies in five holes, then exploded into brilliance as the Northern Irishman is wont to do. He cannot help himself, however disciplined he is trying to be. On the way home, the more difficult holes needed to be negotiated. Hovland got up and down from behind the 17th green and kept his bogey-free card intact.

Scoring was at its easiest of the week so far, but only one player managed not to drop a stroke and that was Hovland when the late starters had to deal with the least favourable conditions. It had been sunny and calm first thing, which Kevin Kisner enjoyed. The American birdied seven of the first 10 holes to jump from a tie for 66th — on the cut line after making a birdie at the 18th late on Friday night — to a tie for 13th and a lie-in for Sunday. His 65 held up as the best score of the day, numerically at least.

There was a 66 for Tommy Fleetwood as he improved by three strokes for the second day running, and the Southport man, runner-up to Shane Lowry at Royal Portrush in 2019, was joined on nine under par by US Open champion Matt Fitzpatrick and Australia's Adam Scott on his 42nd birthday. Lowry had been the first Irishman to excite the gallery at the loop when he chipped in twice in a row for eagle twos at the ninth

McIlroy and Hovland leave the first tee at the start of a magical afternoon.

All smiles for US Open champion Matt Fitzpatrick with three birdies in a row from the ninth during his third round of 69.

Kevin Kisner birdied seven of the first 10 holes in his 65.

South Africa's Dylan Frittelli eagled both the ninth and 18th.

and 10th holes. South Africa's Dylan Frittelli also collected two eagles, at the ninth and the 18th. Time and again scorecards showed lots of lovely red numbers on the way out, then more ugly ones coming home. The inward half averaged almost two shots harder than the outward nine.

McIlroy filled in time in the morning watching the rugby, especially Ireland's historic series-winning victory over the All Blacks in New Zealand. Perhaps Smith stuck with watching *Peaky Blinders*, his current box set of choice, rather than England's win in Australia, but perhaps not. After the long wait for the leaders to tee-off in the third round, something extraordinary happened. Smith missed a four-footer on the first green for his par. Had the putter that had worked miracles over the first two days used up all its magic? Slowly, it began to look that way. Chances he would have taken in the earlier rounds slipped by. He lipped out at the seventh after a fine approach. Not until the ninth did he recover the shot dropped at the first. Alongside him, Young was not faring much better, level par for his first eight holes.

By now the focus had switched to the game ahead of them. Hovland, at 24, is as fearless a putter as they come, and it was the Norwegian who found the secret to Saturday's greens. He holed from 38 feet at the third

and from 42 feet at the fourth for the first two of four birdies in a row. The first player from his country to win on both the PGA and DP World Tours, Hovland's recent form had been patchy. He had missed the cut in his last two starts, the US Open and the Genesis Scottish Open, and for all the promise of the world number nine, he had yet to fire in major championships, his best result being 12th at the 2019 US Open and on his debut in The Open in 2021. With his preparations on the Old Course beginning two days earlier than planned the previous weekend, he found time to play a round at Carnoustie on Monday evening on the basis that it was his caddie's favourite course.

At the par-five fifth, he got a kind bounce with his second and faced a 52-footer for an eagle. This was one not to drop but he tapped in for a four and then made a 20-footer at the sixth. He was now leading The Open by two. McIlroy, after another slowish start, got his birdie at the fifth and also a three at the sixth after the sort of controlled, spin-reducing wedge shot to five feet that he had been working on for just such occasions.

Onto the loop they came, McIlroy seeking that first major title for eight years, Hovland to become only the second golfer from Norway to win a major after

Tommy Fleetwood, with a 66, improved by three strokes for the second day in a row.

Out at the loop, McIlroy's drive at the ninth set up a birdie.

Suzann Pettersen. "To win the major closest to home, the one I always watched growing up, would be really cool," Hovland said. "It's pretty crazy from where I grew up so far away from the PGA Tour, the DP World Tour, for that matter major championships, so it is special to be here and to have a chance. Norway has always been a winter nation and done well at the Olympics, but now we have a bunch of good athletes coming up in summer sports as well. The support I've seen in Norway the last couple of years is really cool."

But nothing like the support being shown to McIlroy out at the loop. "I had some experience with that at the Ryder Cup last year," Hovland said. "I don't mind. There were still some shouts for me." Hovland saved par at the eighth with two good putts from off the left side of the green, then three-putted the ninth for a par. McIlroy got his three at the ninth, to be one behind, and then found the little circular bunker in front of the 10th green with his next drive.

Twice McIlroy had to back off his bunker shot as play continued in close proximity all around. His ball was right in the centre of the sand, the hole 27 yards away on a raised tier. "It was perched on a little crown,"

Scott still keeping the Claret Jug dream alive

Adam Scott was serenaded by the crowd on his 42nd birthday as he posted a 70 to be inside the top 10 at nine under par.

The Australian would have given much for the 66 he scored on his birthday at Royal St George's in 2021, or the 65 he returned in the second round this year. But he drove into a bunker at the fourth, did well to get away with a bogey, and never got going. "I was just a hair off," Scott said. "It didn't go my way over the first few holes. That has to change tomorrow if I want to dream of playing with

anything on the line on the back nine."

Scott was still hankering for the Claret Jug he came so close to winning at Royal Lytham & St Annes 10 years earlier. Had he won, he would have been playing in The R&A Celebration of Champions rather than watching it from a grandstand, but it was still a highlight of the week for the 2013 Masters champion. "To sit on a nice day at St Andrews on the Road Hole and watch all the past Champions come by, I don't know if there's a greater way of appreciating golf and the Championship's history than that," he said. "It was a fun afternoon." Lee Trevino was of particular interest to Scott. "To watch him strike it was fantastic. He's about the only legend that I've not played with and we are hoping to play at some point."

As for the Old Course, Scott felt the auld lady was holding her own. "This is just a wee breeze, it's no wind, but it's firming up. I think they have done a good job setting it up. They've gone about as extreme as they can without being silly on the pins. If 20 under par wins tomorrow, that's not an embarrassment at all. That's what wins most golf tournaments we play these days."

Hovland wielded his putter to magnificent effect with four birdies in a row.

Adam Scott was "just a hair off" as he found bunker trouble on his 42nd birthday.

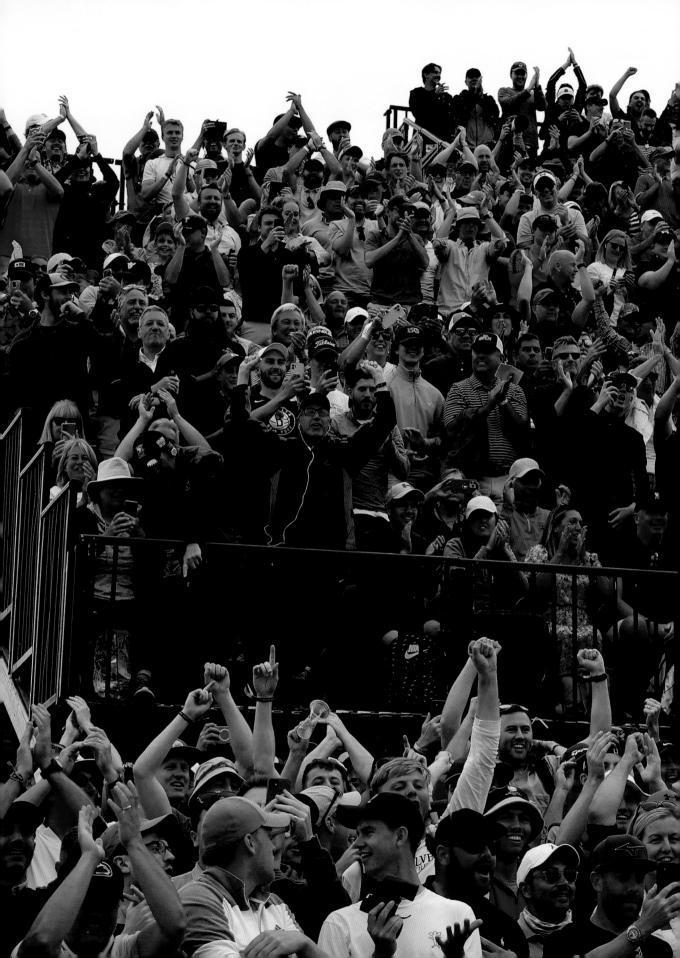

Fans in the grandstand react as McIlroy holes his second shot from a bunker on the 10th hole.

EXCERPTS FROM THE PRESS

"Rory has talked this week about playing boring golf to try and land his dream of winning The Open at St Andrews. But there was nothing boring about the way The Open winner at Hoylake in 2014 approached his task on moving day."

—Adam Lanigan,
Sunday Post

"If the 24-year-old Hovland were to claim the Claret Jug, it would mark the first time that the four majors were all won by players under 30."

—Adam Schupak,
Golfweek

"The record crowds who have flocked to St Andrews for this historic Open have made no secret that McIlroy is their favourite. That bias is palpable every step of the way from the town to the loop and back again."

—Scott Michaux
Irish Examiner

"Fleetwood is a player who often rises to the occasion, yet so far has been unable to string together four consecutive rounds that are good enough to land the ultimate prize."

—Stuart Fraser,
The Sunday Times

"One unlucky roll on the back nine cost Scottie Scheffler a couple of strokes and plenty of momentum."

—Chris Lehourites,
Associated Press

"Too much can be made of pairings but there is no doubt McIlroy and Hovland fed off each other's sparkling play."

—Andy Dunn,
Sunday People

Hovland was attempting to become the first male major winner from Norway.

Spain's Jon Rahm rues a bogey at the second hole on the way to a 71.

Shane Lowry checks his course notes during a rollercoaster round of 69.

McIlroy acknowledges the huge ovation sparked by his brilliant shot from a bunker for an eagle at the 10th hole.

McIlroy said. "I was just trying to get it somewhat close. Anything inside 10 feet was going to be a really good shot. It just came out perfectly." He carried his ball onto the tier and then saw it run inexorably into the hole. "I think that's the first bunker I put it in this week. And it was a nice result. It was skill to put it somewhere close, but it was luck that it went in. You need a little bit of luck now and again, especially in the big tournaments. That was a nice bonus." Or, as Hovland put it, "Disregarding the situation, that's just a filthy bunker shot. That was sick."

Hovland then holed a second putt of 14 feet for a birdie and the pair were tied at 15 under par. McIlroy briefly punched the air when his shot went in, and the crowd went crazy, but did not celebrate quite as extravagantly as at the 72nd hole of the Masters Tournament when he made a walk-off hole-out. This time he was being courteous to other players — Scheffler and Johnson were hitting their tee shots at the 11th — and aware of how much work remained for the day and the Championship.

At the par-five 14th, McIlroy launched his second from over on the fifth fairway 277 yards to pin high on the green and two-putted for birdie. With Hovland failing to get up and down from in front of the green, at 7.17pm McIlroy now led The Open on his own. Back towards the town he came, the roars increasing with every step. The 16th and the 17th were the hardest two holes on the course. Hovland holed a six-footer to save par at 16, then both faced approaches from the left rough at the 17th.

With the hole located behind the Road Hole bunker, only 8.4 per cent of the field found the green in regulation in the third round. Neither of this pair were among them. Hovland went straight at the flag, and finished over the back on the path in front of the road. McIlroy played more conservatively but got a flier, his ball ricocheting back off the wall at the back. He chipped on and took two putts for his only bogey of the day. Hovland was able to putt. "I felt that was the safest play," he said. "It came out exactly perfect." He only had four feet left for his par and made that, so the pair were tied again.

Birdies for each at the 18th was a fitting finale to the round. "That was pretty cool, I'm not going to forget this day too quickly," Hovland said after posting his fifth consecutive round under 70 in The Open. Going back to his debut at Royal St George's he had scored six of his seven Open rounds under 70. Another would be welcome the next day when he would be alongside McIlroy again in the last pairing. "There's a lot of things that can happen," he said. "It depends on the conditions, the pin locations and, frankly, how we play."

"We fed off each other and navigated the tricky holes coming in," McIlroy said. "I missed some

Round of the Day: **Rory McIlroy - 66**

Round of the Day: **Viktor Hovland - 66**

Amateur Aaron Jarvis was the first player from the Cayman Islands to play in The Open.

Eagle-two lands twice for Lowry

As one writer put it so succinctly: "It's easy to find history at St Andrews, but it's nearly impossible to make it. In order to make history here, one has to outlast the ghosts of golf's past — and there are a lot of them."

All credit then to Shane Lowry, the Irishman who lifted the Claret Jug in spectacular fashion at Royal Portrush in 2019, for stamping another mark on golf's original championship. With a short game seemingly forged by the golfing gods, he became the first player since Phil Mickelson at Royal Lytham & St Annes in 2001 to have consecutive eagles, and the first ever on two par fours.

The first came at the 352-yard ninth, a hole that was within reach for most players. But while Lowry missed the green 25 yards to the right with his first, he found the bottom of the hole with his second. Using a wedge from light rough, he struck the ball perfectly and watched as it bounced three times, applied the brakes, crawled towards the hole and fell in.

At the 10th, Lowry was left with another short wedge shot into the green after a confident drive down the middle of the fairway. This time he hit a low pitch from a bare lie and followed the ball's trajectory as it landed at the front of the green before navigating the bumps and mounds on its way to the hole. As it dropped in, so Lowry put both arms in the air in acknowledgement of the cheers that were ringing in his ears. "It was good fun when those two went in," he said. "But the rest of the day wasn't so enjoyable." Four under par for those two holes, he was one over par the rest of the way for a 69. But as short-game cameos go, this one was up there with the best.

opportunities and was watching Viktor hole a couple of long ones, but feel I was rewarded for my patience around the turn with a couple of birdies and that hole-out on 10. It was really good."

McIlroy's hotel room looked down on the scene at the 18th where his name would sit at the top of the leaderboard all night. A second Claret Jug, eight years after his Hoylake triumph, was within reach, at least in his dreams. "I think it's about appreciating the fact that it's unbelievably cool to have a chance to win The Open at St Andrews. It's what dreams are made of. I'm going to try and make a dream come true tomorrow."

But he cautioned: "The more people bring up the result, the more I'm going to harp on about process and sticking to my game plan. I've done that well for three days and it's put me in this position. I just need to do it for one more day. I can't worry about Viktor, or the two Camerons or whoever. I have to do my thing."

The two Camerons were still coming home, but drifting back. Young had three birdies in four holes from the ninth, but had a double bogey at the 16th after missing the green on the right. Neither he nor Smith birdied the 18th. Smith also had a double, his coming at the 13th. His tee shot ended on the edge of a bunker and, with his feet in the sand, Smith tried to play a waist high shot that never had a chance to carry the wild terrain in front of the green. He took two more hacks in the heather and two putts for a six.

"I thought I could do it, get it over the stuff and somewhere left of the pin, but obviously not," Smith said of the second shot. He added: "The golfing gods weren't with me today. I felt as if I hit a lot of good putts, just nothing was really dropping. The opposite to the first two days, which is pretty hard to take on the chin." He did get up and down neatly from the left of the 17th green, otherwise he may have fallen too far back.

Saturday had seen a duel to remember at St Andrews. But was there any guarantee that the same two players would fire together on Sunday? At four strokes behind, The Players champion would have to chase hard the next day, and then anything might be possible. On reflection, Smith did not mind that. "I love making birdies. I love making putts. That's what I need to go out there and do tomorrow. I need to stay aggressive and make a ton of birdies."

Cameron Smith almost holes his chip from left of the green at the 17th hole.

THIRD ROUND LEADERS

HOLE	1	2	3	4	5	6	7	8	9	OUT	10	11	12	13	14	15	16	17	18	IN	TOTAL
PAR	4	4	4	4	5	4	4	3	4	36	4	3	4	4	5	4	4	4	4	36	72
Viktor Hovland	4	4	3	3	4	3	4	3	4	32	3	3	4	4	5	4	4	4	3	34	66-200
Rory McIlroy	4	4	4	4	4	3	4	3	3	33	2	3	4	4	4	4	4	5	3	33	66-200
Cameron Young	4	4	4	4	4	5	5	3	3	35	3	3	3	5	4	4	6	4	4	36	71-204
Cameron Smith	5	4	4	5	4	4	4	3	3	36	4	3	4	6	4	4	4	4	4	37	73-204
Si Woo Kim	4	4	4	4	4	4	3	3	4	34	3	3	4	4	4	3	5	4	3	33	67-205
Scottie Scheffler	4	4	3	4	4	4	4	3	4	34	3	2	5	4	5	4	4	5	3	35	69-205
Dustin Johnson	4	3	3	5	5	4	4	3	3	34	3	3	4	5	6	4	5	4	3	37	71-206
Tommy Fleetwood	3	3	4	4	4	4	3	4	3	32	4	3	4	3	4	4	4	4	3	34	66-207
Matt Fitzpatrick	4	4	4	5	4	4	4	3	3	36	4	3	4	4	4	4	4	3	3	33	69-207
Adam Scott	4	4	4	5	4	4	5	4	3	37	3	3	4	3	5	4	3	5	3	33	70-207
Jordan Spieth	4	4	3	4	5	4	3	3	3	33	4	3	4	3	5	4	4	5	3	35	68-208
Patrick Cantlay	4	4	3	4	4	3	4	3	3	32	4	3	5	4	5	4	6	4	4	39	71-208

■ EAGLE OR BETTER ■ BIRDIES □ PAR ■ OVER PAR

SCORING SUMMARY

THIRD ROUND SCORES

Players Under Par	45
Players At Par	9
Players Over Par	29

LOW SCORES

Low First Nine

Kevin Kisner	30

Low Second Nine

Matt Fitzpatrick	33
Si Woo Kim	33
Rory McIlroy	33
Adam Scott	33

Low Round

Kevin Kisner	65

THIRD ROUND HOLE SUMMARY

HOLE	PAR	YARDS	EAGLES	BIRDIES	PARS	BOGEYS	D.BOGEYS	OTHER	RANK	AVERAGE
1	4	375	0	18	62	3	0	0	13	3.819
2	4	452	0	10	56	15	2	0	6	4.108
3	4	398	0	25	50	8	0	0	14	3.795
4	4	480	0	4	58	20	1	0	4	4.217
5	5	570	1	40	38	2	2	0	16	4.566
6	4	414	0	17	55	9	1	1	10	3.964
7	4	371	0	19	51	12	1	0	11	3.940
8	3	187	0	4	69	9	0	1	7	3.096
9	4	352	7	50	25	1	0	0	18	3.241
OUT	36	3,599	8	187	464	79	7	2		34.747
10	4	386	2	26	42	13	0	0	14	3.795
11	3	174	0	7	53	21	2	0	4	3.217
12	4	351	0	14	49	18	2	0	7	4.096
13	4	465	0	5	56	19	3	0	3	4.241
14	5	614	0	32	39	6	5	1	12	4.843
15	4	455	0	7	63	13	0	0	9	4.072
16	4	418	0	9	47	20	7	0	2	4.301
17	4	495	0	1	34	44	3	1	1	4.627
18	4	356	2	48	31	2	0	0	17	3.398
IN	36	3,714	4	149	414	156	22	2		36.59
TOTAL	72	7,313	12	336	878	235	29	4		71.337

The Road Hole bites back

Alistair Tait sees the 17th return to its rightful place as the most feared hole in golf

No hole in The Open's pool of courses strikes as much fear into the hearts of would-be Champion Golfers of the Year than the Old Course's 17th, the Road Hole. Ben Crenshaw famously said: "The reason the Road Hole at St Andrews is the greatest par four in the world is because it's actually a par five."

Seve Ballesteros certainly thought so. He didn't make his first par on the 17th during the 1984 Championship until the final round, setting up that iconic victorious moment on the 18th green when he claimed the old Claret Jug for the second time. However, in an earlier round he described his play of the hole thus: "A good tee shot, five-iron, chip and two putts for a par five." When R&A press officer George Simms reminded Seve that the 17th was actually a par four, Seve replied: "For you, George, it may be a par four. For Seve Ballesteros, it's a par five."

Nine shots to play the most feared hole in golf are not uncommon. Mark Calcavecchia, the 1989 Champion Golfer, holed a putt for a nine in the first round of the Championship in 2015. That's the same number Tommy Nakajima made in the third round of The Open in 1978. The Japanese player had a putt for the lead only to send his ball into the Road Hole Bunker. Four sand shots and two putts later, locals were dubbing the hole, "the Sands of Nakajima".

In each of the seven previous Championships at St Andrews since statistical records began in 1982, the Road Hole had topped the list of hardest holes. It played to a stroke average of 4.67 for those seven Championships. It averaged 4.79 strokes in 1984, statistically the hardest hole ever in an Open. Indeed, the 17th had featured six times in the top-10 list of most difficult holes in relation to par since 1982.

Yet after the opening two rounds of this year's Championship, the Road Hole had proved to be more pussycat than screeching Scottish wild cat. The hole yielded 11 birdies on the opening day, two more than the entire total for the 2015 Championship. It played to a stroke average of just 4.39 for the 156 competitors, bettering the previous low stroke average of 4.41 in the

Viktor Hovland managed to save par by two-putting from the path over the green at the Road Hole.

The scene at the 17th as Rory McIlroy chips from over the road on the way to a "Seve par", his only bogey of the third round.

third round of 2015. Moreover, the Road Hole fell off its perch as the Old Course's hardest hole. It ranked third most difficult behind the 13th (4.51) and the fourth (4.43). It was a first for Opens at St Andrews since 1984 that the Road Hole wasn't the most difficult hole.

The 17th regained its status as the hardest hole in round two when it yielded only six birdies. However, it came in at a stroke average of just 4.35, beating round one as the lowest stroke average in an Open since 1984. That soon changed 24 hours later.

Forty-four bogeys were recorded on the hole in round three, while David Carey, Cameron Tringale and Harold Varner III made double bogeys, and Australian Lucas Herbert recorded a seven on his scorecard.

Trey Mullinax made his third straight "Seve par" on the hole, taking a course of action the maestro described in 1984. Rather than flirt with the Road Hole bunker, the American decided to "aim 20 yards left of the green, hope it stays out of the water, and run it up." It was a new experience for the one-time PGA Tour winner: "I've never played 20 yards away from a green," he admitted.

Mullinax returned a relatively comfortable six-under-par 66, punctuated by that lone bogey.

"Seventeen was the only real grind we had out there today," he said.

Ditto for joint 54-hole leader Rory McIlroy, who also returned a 66. He, too, made a "Seve par" on the 17th, and was pleased to do so. McIlroy had 127 yards to the front of the green, and was trying to land his ball 135 yards only to see it end up close to the wall beyond the road that gives the hole its name.

"It could have been way worse," McIlroy said. "It could have been up against the wall. It could have been anywhere. So to chip it onto the green and take two putts, I was happy enough to get out of there with a five."

So were many of the rest of the field. When the sun set on the third round of The 150th Open, the Road Hole had returned to its rightful place as the most feared hole in major championship golf. Justin Thomas was the only player of the 83 competitors to birdie the 17th. The stroke average jumped to 4.63, the hardest hole on the course by a third of a stroke over the 16th.

And, on Sunday, the 71st hole of the Championship was once again critical to its outcome. Somewhere up in that great clubhouse in the sky, Seve Ballesteros and the other gods of golf were smiling.

SUBLIME SMITH'S VICTORY FOR OZ

By Andy Farrell

When Cameron Smith said he loved making putts and he loved making birdies, well, he meant it. What a place to prove it, on the back nine of the Old Course in the final round of The 150th Open. Five birdies in a row and another on the 18th green. He had talked the talk, then he got to walk the walk of the Champion Golfer of the Year, with the Claret Jug in his hands.

There is magic in those hands, at least the way the 28-year-old Australian wielded the flat stick over these four days. From the turn on Sunday, this putting wizard of Oz went to a new level. In the previous 149 Championships, no one had played the last nine holes in as few as 30 strokes to win. Nothing less was good enough for Smith to defeat Cameron Young by one and Rory McIlroy by two strokes.

"Golf's Holy Grail", McIlroy had called winning The Open at St Andrews. McIlroy's noble quest was thwarted only by the brilliance of Smith and a stunning eagle at the last from Young. For two-thirds of the afternoon McIlroy led. But it was incredibly tense. As he had been all week, McIlroy was the favourite of the huge gallery. He hardly did anything wrong, but it was Smith who found the spark of genius under pressure. And it wasn't all about the birdies, his brave two-putt around the Road Hole bunker for a vital par at the 17th no less vital to the outcome.

"I feel like I can breathe," Smith gasped, almost an hour after completing his second 64 of the week. "Those last four or five holes aren't easy around here, especially with the wind up off the left. I'm just proud of how I knuckled down and managed to get it done."

He was the third Australian to win at the home of

golf. The late Peter Thomson, whose ashes were scattered in a corner of the 18th green on the morning of this final round, was the first in 1955. His contemporary Kel Nagle then won the 100th anniversary Open in 1960. Nagle, with an important putt at the 17th, held off Arnold Palmer, the winner of that year's first two majors and the crowd favourite. Eerie how history repeats itself. Greg Norman, twice, and Ian Baker-Finch are the only two other Champion Golfers from Australia.

"To win an Open Championship in itself is probably going to be a golfer's highlight in their career," Smith said. "To do it around St Andrews, I think it's just unbelievable. This place is so cool. I love the golf course. I love the town." Looking at the Claret Jug, he added: "All the names on there, every player that's been at the top of their game has won this Championship. It hasn't really sunk in yet. It's just unreal." He told the crowd: "This one's for Oz."

On the three previous occasions, in four attempts, that Smith had made the cut at The Open, he had not fared better on a Sunday than the 74 he scored at Royal St George's in 2021. This time it was the third round on Saturday that looked the ridiculous outlier, the man from Down Under returning to his sublime best for the final day. With rounds of 67-64-73-64, Smith set a new record total for Opens at St Andrews of 268, beating the 269 of Tiger Woods in 2000, while his score of 20 under par tied Henrik Stenson's record at Royal Troon in 2016.

Smith had been the first player to score four rounds in the 60s in the Masters Tournament at Augusta National in 2020. But he had not won, finishing runner-up. The major near-misses were mounting up. In 2022 he finished third at Augusta, unable to put

Cameron Smith taps in for victory at The 150th Open.

pressure on Scottie Scheffler during the final round. McIlroy had stolen second place on that occasion with his dramatic bunker hole-out at the final hole.

That was McIlroy's best major finish of 2022 yet it actually came while he never felt in contention for the Green Jacket. That was not the case at St Andrews, as his name sat alongside Viktor Hovland's at the top of the giant yellow scoreboards at the 18th all Saturday night and Sunday morning. Amid the early morning showers, Sam Burns turned in a 64 with birdies at the last four holes. Was it remotely possible someone could do that later in the day with the breeze up?

Italy's Filippo Celli secured the Silver Medal for the leading amateur ahead of Aaron Jarvis, Barclay Brown and Sam Bairstow, while Thailand's Sadom Kaewkanjana scored a 65 to finish 11th, the highest by anyone from his country at The Open. Tommy Fleetwood scored a 67 to move to 14 under par and eventually a share of fourth place. Scheffler and Si Woo Kim, playing together, both had a chance to post four rounds in the 60s, but each fell back into the 70s. So did the other pair of players who had the same opportunity — McIlroy and Hovland in the final game.

It was the first time in eight rounds in The Open at St Andrews that McIlroy had scored in the 70s. (He also has a score of 80 from the second round of 2010 on his record.) His round now of two birdies and 16 pars — against a new record low scoring average for the day of 69.68 — included hitting all 18 greens in regulation and taking 36 putts. Hovland dropped to a 74 and down into a share of fourth with Fleetwood.

They simply did not push each other on. It had happened the day before to Saturday's final pairing of the two Camerons. Any suggestion of a continuation of the McIlroy-Hovland dramatics for the full weekend slowly fizzled out. Smith and Young, playing together again but this time in the penultimate game four strokes behind the leaders, eventually took their places.

It took a while to reveal itself, this final round. McIlroy's putt at the first green rolled over the left edge of the hole. That was to happen a lot, but at this stage it was no bother. He missed a good chance at the third from five feet. Same thing. Hovland three-putted the fourth to fall one behind. McIlroy went in front by two with a two-putt birdie at the fifth which the Norwegian could not match.

"I could have got some momentum going if I made a few more putts early, but at the same time, I just made a few too many errors," said Hovland, who was seeking

IT'S A FACT

Ahead of the final round, four players had the chance to complete four rounds under 70, but none achieved the feat. So Viktor Hovland's run of five rounds in the 60s, dating back to the third round in 2021, came to an end. The record for most consecutive rounds under 70 is seven, recorded by Ernie Els from round one of 1993 to round three of 1994. Nick Price and Henrik Stenson both recorded six consecutive rounds under 70.

A 65 for Thailand's Sadom Kaewkanjana as he finished in a tie for 11th place.

Tommy Fleetwood, assessing his approach shot at the 13th hole, moved up into a tie for fourth with a 67.

Bryson DeChambeau, teeing off at the second hole, saved his best for last as a 66 took him into a tie for eighth place.

EXCERPTS FROM THE PRESS

"Acts of gatecrashing rarely come in a form as outrageous or as painful as this. For Stewart Cink and the Turnberry torment of 2009, read Australian Cameron Smith and the St Andrews steal at The 150th Open."

—Derek Lawrenson,
Daily Mail

"The knee-knocking putt around the Road Hole bunker which produced an incredible par save on the 17th will be the stroke he will remember for a long time, snaking along the camber and giving the kid from Wantima Country Club a makeable par putt."

—Adam Pengilly,
Brisbane Times

"Miss it on 17, and make a four at the last, and likely it wouldn't be enough. But the Queenslander is the best putter in the game — his work on the greens in Scotland was ridiculous — and he rolled his ball into the dead middle of the hole."

—Mike Clayton,
Australian Golf Media

"The fearless, unyielding Young, making his Open debut, conjured a jaw-dropping finish with a two on the last."

—Nick Rodger,
The Herald

"If ever an Open Championship, if ever a setting merited the kind of golf played by Smith, it is the oldest major in the sport at the course where it all started."

—Kevin Garside,
i newspaper

A final round of 66 took Brian Harman, teeing off on 17, into a tie for sixth.

Out of position for a bogey at the second, Patrick Cantlay rallied for a 68.

to become the first male major champion from Norway. "It was a little anti-climactic after yesterday. I was expecting to hang in there for a bit longer, but I just didn't have it today."

Hovland got to the turn without making a birdie, and made only one for the day, at the 12th. McIlroy kept giving himself chances, but at the sixth and the ninth his ball slid by again.

Smith had stopped at the putting green late on Saturday night, just to see the ball going in the hole again after a third round when his putter had been uncharacteristically cool. "It turned out it was a pretty good thing to do," he said. "Today I went out there to stick my head down and keep making putts and keep making birdies."

He started at the second, from eight feet. Then he two-putted from 88 feet for a four at the fifth. He was two behind then, but with McIlroy also birdieing the fifth, Smith reached the turn three behind, a good chance lipping out at the ninth. Young had bogeyed the first, hit back with four birdies in five holes from the third, then drove into the gorse at the ninth. He took relief and ended up with another bogey so both he and Smith were out in 34, just one shot knocked off their overnight deficit.

"I knew I had to be patient," Smith said. "I felt good all day. When those putts started going in on the back nine, it gave me a lot of momentum."

He was just short at the 10th and played the most delightful chip, off one mound and then another, to five feet. He holed that for the first of what would be five in a row. At the dangerous 11th, he hit a nine-iron

Dustin Johnson, in the top 10 on the leaderboard all week, closed with a 69 for a share of sixth place.

almost pin high to the hole at the back of the green. A 16-footer went in there. "When that one dropped, I could see the hole getting a lot bigger, for sure."

At the 12th, Smith threaded his drive between the mounds and the big bunker onto the front of the green, then putted up the tier to 11 feet and made that one. With McIlroy having two-putted the 10th from long range for his second and last birdie of the round, Smith was still one behind. That soon changed. A drive and a sawn-off six-iron, from 187 yards, did not just find the heart of the 13th green, but put him within 18 feet of the hole. "Those two shots were two of the best all week," he said. "My second shot was when I thought we could really win this thing."

Holing the putt put him to 18 under par and tied for the lead with McIlroy. Two big blows at the par-five 14th put Smith just off the back of the green. He then hit the most gorgeous lag putt, from almost 30 yards, to within tap-in range. He now led by one at 19 under par.

Young, refusing to back off despite the onslaught, had also birdied the 10th, the 13th, with a fine approach shot of his own, and the 14th to be two behind. McIlroy went close at 12, saw his putt at 13 pull up just short of the hole, and then took three putts from short of the 14th green. He was trying to stay patient, the crowd were still supportive, but the final game had developed a subdued air.

Now, until the final hole, it was about the pars, not the birdies. Smith survived a leaked drive into the right rough at the 15th, holing a good second putt for the par. Young needed a good two-putt at the 16th. McIlroy remained unscathed but still one back.

As ever, this 30th staging of The Open at St Andrews remained in doubt through at least the 71st hole. The Road Hole was back to its fiercest over the weekend and Smith's second shot with a nine-iron stalled at the front of the green, running off to the left to leave the bunker between himself and the flagstick. "I didn't commit to the draw shape I wanted, got it a little bit toey, and turned it over a little more than I would have liked," he explained.

At the point of maximum danger, Smith relied on his putter. He swung the first effort off the contours to the right of the bunker, within two feet of the cliff face, and onto the green, 10 feet right of the hole. "I was just trying to get it within 15 feet, somewhere in there where I'd be able to give it a pretty good run. Managed to get away with a four."

Young said: "For him to accept he was going to have a 10-12-footer for par, obviously he hit a great first putt. There was no guarantee of having a par putt that short. It's another example of why he is one of the very

Viktor Hovland fell out of the lead with a three-putt bogey at the fourth hole as the Norwegian's challenge faded on Sunday.

Early in the final round, Rory McIlroy looked as commanding as ever as he moved into a two-stroke lead.

Celli claims the Silver Medal for Italy

In years to come Filippo Celli will recount his week at St Andrews and reflect on the four exceptional rounds of golf that brought him the Silver Medal as leading amateur at The 150th Open. The Italian will recall how he had rounds of 74-67-71-71 over the Old Course to be five under par and finish six shots clear of his nearest rival, Aaron Jarvis, of the Cayman Islands.

Likely to be given equal billing when it comes to telling his story, however, will be the impromptu practice round he ended up sharing with his idol,

Rory McIlroy, having met the four-time major champion for the first time on the shared fifth and 13th green during Monday's practice. "I was so happy when Rory turned to face me and my caddie, Alberto, and he asked, 'hey, guys, do you mind if I join you for the back nine?' I looked at Alberto, I say, he's serious or not? I say, 'Rory, of course you can.'

"I was so lucky and happy because it's a dream come true. I grew up watching the videos and the wins of Rory, all the stuff that he won. So, it's amazing. I'm feeling very happy and proud. I can't ask for a better thing than to win the Silver Medal at The 150th Open in St Andrews."

Celli all but sealed the prize with an eagle at the par-five 14th in the final round following a superb approach shot and a routine putt. He then completed proceedings with a birdie at the last — his fourth in four days at the same hole — to spark tears of joy from his parents watching beside the green.

This was a strong championship for the amateurs. Of the six who started the week, four made the halfway cut. England's Barclay Brown, who led the way with a first round of 68, finished in a tie for 79th on two over par, while his compatriot Sam Bairstow, 23, was two shots further back in a tie for 81st.

Smith putts his way out of trouble at the Road Hole, skirting the dangerous bunker and setting up a vital par.

best. He made a really good decision and executed it perfectly."

Young himself had hit a superb second shot, finishing in a similar position but missed his birdie putt, just as surely as Smith holed his for par. The Australian was not giving an inch, and now McIlroy was forced to deliver. His approach at the 17th certainly did, accompanied by another huge roar for Rors, but while his 18-footer was perfect for length, it was a couple of inches to the left. There had been 22 birdies at the 17th during The 150th Open, more than ever before, but what the Northern Irishman would have given for making it 23.

When Smith birdied the 18th, McIlroy needed a two to tie. His drive came up short and he needed to chip over the Valley of Sin, the ball running 20 feet past the hole. Yet another two-putt par and the dream of a first major title for eight years dashed. "It's one I feel I let slip away," McIlroy said. "The putter went a little cold today. I played a controlled round of golf, didn't do too much wrong, but didn't do too much right either.

"I'll rue a few missed putts, but, look, I got beaten by a better player this week. Twenty under par for four rounds of golf around here is really impressive, especially that 64 today to get it done. I can't be too despondent. I'm playing some of the best golf I've played in a long time. It's a matter of keep knocking on the door, eventually one will open."

Cameron Young tangles with the gorse at the ninth hole.

Smith drives at the 18th hole.

Of the nine players who made the cut in all four major championships in 2022, McIlroy was eight shots ahead of Will Zalatoris at 29 under par. Only Matt Fitzpatrick and Justin Thomas also finished the year under par. He left with the roars from the fans still ringing in his ears, something he fully appreciated. They love him because he admits he dares to dream. "I'm only human. I'm not a robot," he said. On the buggy ferrying him away at the end, his wife cradled his head on her shoulder.

Smith admitted he had never dreamed as far as winning the Claret Jug at the home of golf. There was still almost a rude awakening from his playing partner. Young, who came to the 18th still two behind Smith,

had one last surprise on his debut Open, driving the green and holing the 17-foot putt for an eagle, a 65 and second place. "You obviously never know, so I was trying to give myself some sort of look. But based on how he was playing and how the hole sets up, I thought there was a very good chance that two was not going to be enough."

It wasn't. Smith had driven just in front of the green and lagged delicately round the top of the Valley of Sin to within two feet of the hole. The last two holes on the Old Course are a great combination because each is a half-par hole, the 17th averaged 4.5 for the week, the 18th at 3.5, and Smith went par-birdie just when he needed to.

Front-row seat for runner-up Young

The history of The Open is littered with first-round leaders famous for being just that. Cameron Young, who topped the leaderboard by two on Thursday, never faded from the limelight for four days and almost became famous for being the first player to win The Open at St Andrews on debut since Tony Lema in 1964.

An eagle at the last hole (left, top) meant he finished as runner-up to Cameron Smith by one stroke. It was his fourth second-place finish of his rookie PGA Tour season and improved on his best major finish of third at the PGA Championship in May.

"It probably hurts a little worse to come up one shot short," admitted the 25-year-old New Yorker. "If you lose by eight you don't really care. But I played well today. I would have signed up for a 65 this morning. To watch Cameron shoot what he did, it was pretty amazing. I had a front-row seat to I'm sure one of the better rounds that's been played this year."

Young and Smith started the final round four strokes off the lead and the American had to hang on to the Australian's coat-tails as Smith made five birdies in a row to start the back nine. "Watching him make a million birdies in a row in a sense was good because it pushes you, and in another it's hard to watch because you know he's kind of beating you.

"I said at the PGA, one of these times I'll shoot five under par on the back and that will be enough," Young added. "And today I did. And it wasn't. So I guess one of these times I'll shoot six under on the back on Sunday and that will be enough."

McIlroy's putter went cold on Sunday, including at the 13th (top) and 17th (middle) holes.

"Yet as the hopes and roars got going, so did a trend: McIlroy kept hitting greens but not near holes. He lost the lead despite never really losing his way."

—Chuck Culpepper,
Washington Post

"This was a day when a man with a mullet took a mallet to the Old Course."

—Rick Broadbent,
The Times

"The man who prefers a rod and reel in his hand instead of a nine-iron unleashed the most powerful weapon of the day — his putter."

—Steve DiMeglio,
USA Today

"McIlroy came as close as a player could to winning a major without actually winning the major. He won't get a trophy for that. But it's still true."

—Michael Rosenberg,
Sports Illustrated

"Smith stormed home in 30 — the first time that has happened in an Open at St Andrews since McIlroy in 2010. Oh, the irony."

—Martin Dempster,
The Scotsman

"There are times when you can only tip your cap and say, 'fair dinkum'. For McIlroy this was one of these. Cameron Smith won this, McIlroy did not lose it."

—James Corrigan,
The Daily Telegraph

McIlroy on the 18th green as the final game putts out at the conclusion of The 150th Open.

Round of the Day: Cameron Smith - 64

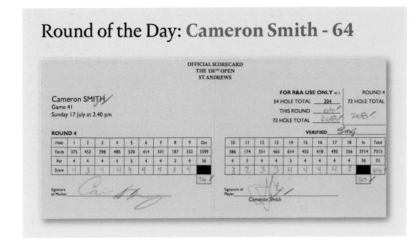

For the first time since the Masters Tournament started in 1934, there were four different winners of the men's professional majors all in their 20s — Scheffler (25, Masters), Thomas (29, PGA Championship), Fitzpatrick (27, US Open) and Smith (28). The Queenslander started playing golf aged two at Wantima Country Club, in the northern suburbs of Brisbane, where his dad Des was the club captain. Des Smith was due to be at St Andrews but decided not to make the trip at the last minute. "He's definitely kicking himself now," Cam said.

At the start of 2022, Smith, for all his undoubted promise and pedigree, had won only three times on the PGA Tour, twice at the Zurich Classic pairs event. "That made me more eager to knuckle down this year and try to get over the line." He made a good start by winning the Sentry Tournament of Champions in January and then The Players Championship in March. Now here. "For it to happen three times this year is pretty unreal," Smith said. "I would have been happy with one."

Only Jack Nicklaus had previously won The Players and The Open in the same year. Only Smith had done it at the Stadium Course at TPC Sawgrass and the Old Course at St Andrews. "There's not a lot of similarities, to be honest," Smith said. "When Sawgrass plays firm and fast, it can be similar in some aspects. But they are two really different golf courses. I think you have to be two completely different golfers to contend at both of those courses."

Or one great one who loves making putts and loves making birdies. That works pretty much anywhere. It is certainly what it took to win as glorious a championship as The 150th Open turned out to be.

The new Champion Golfer of the Year poses for the cameras with the Claret Jug after telling the crowd: "This one's for Oz."

Smith and his caddie, Sam Pinfold, walk down the 18th fairway with the Claret Jug still to be won.

FOURTH ROUND LEADERS

HOLE	1	2	3	4	5	6	7	8	9	OUT	10	11	12	13	14	15	16	17	18	IN	TOTAL
PAR	4	4	4	4	5	4	4	3	4	36	4	3	4	4	5	4	4	4	4	36	72
Cameron Smith	4	3	4	4	4	4	4	3	4	34	3	2	3	3	4	4	4	4	3	30	64-268
Cameron Young	5	4	3	3	4	4	3	3	5	34	3	3	4	3	4	4	4	4	2	31	65-269
Rory McIlroy	4	4	4	4	4	4	4	3	4	35	3	4	4	4	5	4	4	4	3	35	70-270
Tommy Fleetwood	3	4	4	4	4	4	3	3	4	33	4	3	4	4	4	4	4	4	3	34	67-274
Viktor Hovland	4	4	4	5	5	4	4	3	4	37	4	3	3	5	5	4	5	4	4	37	74-274
Brian Harman	4	4	3	3	5	4	3	3	3	32	4	3	5	4	5	3	3	4	3	34	66-275
Dustin Johnson	4	3	4	4	5	4	3	3	4	34	4	2	4	4	5	3	4	5	4	35	69-275
Bryson DeChambeau	4	4	4	5	4	4	3	3	4	35	3	3	3	5	4	4	3	3	3	31	66-276
Patrick Cantlay	4	5	3	4	3	4	5	3	5	36	4	2	3	5	4	4	3	4	3	32	68-276
Jordan Spieth	4	3	3	4	4	4	3	4	4	33	3	3	4	4	6	3	4	4	4	35	68-276

■ EAGLE OR BETTER   ■ BIRDIES   ☐ PAR   ■ OVER PAR

SCORING SUMMARY

FOURTH ROUND SCORES

Players Under Par	61
Players At Par	4
Players Over Par	18

CHAMPIONSHIP SCORES

Rounds Under Par	236
Rounds At Par	49
Rounds Over Par	193

LOW SCORES

Low First Nine

Dean Burmester	32
Brian Harman	32
Sadom Kaewkanjana	32
Chris Kirk	32
Kevin Kisner	32

Low Second Nine

Cameron Smith	30

Low Round

Sam Burns	64
Cameron Smith	64

FOURTH ROUND HOLE SUMMARY

HOLE	PAR	YARDS	EAGLES	BIRDIES	PARS	BOGEYS	D.BOGEYS	OTHER	RANK	AVERAGE
1	4	375	0	7	66	9	1	0	4	4.048
2	4	452	0	14	57	11	1	0	6	3.988
3	4	398	0	32	45	6	0	0	14	3.687
4	4	480	0	7	60	13	3	0	2	4.145
5	5	570	6	45	27	5	0	0	18	4.373
6	4	414	0	20	56	7	0	0	10	3.843
7	4	371	0	23	55	5	0	0	12	3.783
8	3	187	0	11	66	6	0	0	7	2.940
9	4	352	1	32	42	8	0	0	14	3.687
OUT	36	3,599	7	191	474	70	5	0		34.494
10	4	386	0	29	53	1	0	0	16	3.663
11	3	174	0	5	70	7	1	0	4	3.048
12	4	351	1	24	48	9	1	0	11	3.819
13	4	465	0	11	54	17	1	0	3	4.096
14	5	614	6	30	33	11	2	1	13	4.711
15	4	455	0	17	56	9	1	0	8	3.928
16	4	418	0	20	51	12	0	0	9	3.904
17	4	495	0	4	39	27	12	1	1	4.602
18	4	356	3	43	37	0	0	0	17	3.410
IN	36	3,714	10	183	441	93	18	2		35.181
TOTAL	72	7,313	17	374	915	163	23	2		69.675

Three back with nine holes to go, I really needed to make something happen.
—**Cameron Smith**

Of course, you have to let yourself dream. My hotel room is directly opposite the big yellow scoreboard, you envision your name at the top. At the start of today, it was at the top, tomorrow, it won't be.
—**Rory McIlroy**

Cam is a worthy Champion. It's unbelievable how he is able to get the ball in the hole.
—**Viktor Hovland**

It's always nice to finish that way. A lot better than yesterday. It's just unfortunate to shoot 64 in the final round and still finish 42nd.
—**Sam Burns**

The crowds have been fantastic, cheering everyone on and creating a really special atmosphere to play in. It's been a great experience as a player.
—**Tyrrell Hatton**

Rory is just a kid who's really good at golf. He's like all the rest of us, really. I think all the fans can relate with him.
—**Marcus Armitage**

The week's been just incredible. Such a special place. My first time around St Andrews. The golf course has stood the test of time.
—**Corey Conners**

Everyone back home in Poland is quite excited. It's part of my job to grow the game. The more I play in these big events, the more people will watch.
—**Adrian Meronk**

Today Thongchai Jaidee watched me so that is special for me. To finish good in a major gives me confidence. I want the Thai people to be proud of me.
—**Sadom Kaewkanjana**

Just walking down the 18th hole today, that's a piece of history, something I will never forget.
—**Jordan Smith**

THE OPEN.COM

I love these weeks. It's what I play golf for. It's what I get out of bed in the morning for. I'll be counting down the months to the Masters.
—**Shane Lowry**

I always get excited for The Open. Hoylake next year, I'm one of the lucky few that can have it close to a home event. That will be special for me.
—**Tommy Fleetwood**

CHAMPIONSHIP HOLE SUMMARY

HOLE	PAR	YARDS	EAGLES	BIRDIES	PARS	BOGEYS	D.BOGEYS	OTHER	RANK	AVERAGE
1	4	375	0	80	339	49	9	1	10	3.979
2	4	452	0	62	301	100	14	1	6	4.144
3	4	398	0	116	312	43	7	0	12	3.877
4	4	480	0	31	299	136	11	1	3	4.272
5	5	570	14	211	212	35	6	0	16	4.598
6	4	414	0	76	324	69	8	1	9	4.025
7	4	371	0	98	333	45	2	0	11	3.897
8	3	187	0	44	356	76	1	1	8	3.077
9	4	352	15	211	214	37	0	1	17	3.579
OUT	**36**	**3,599**	**29**	**929**	**2,690**	**590**	**58**	**6**		**35.45**
10	4	386	2	137	293	46	0	0	14	3.801
11	3	174	0	30	331	100	14	3	4	3.224
12	4	351	4	148	247	67	10	2	13	3.868
13	4	465	0	24	304	132	18	0	2	4.301
14	5	614	11	187	214	55	9	2	15	4.728
15	4	455	1	50	330	96	1	0	7	4.096
16	4	418	0	58	292	107	18	3	5	4.197
17	4	495	0	22	257	163	31	5	1	4.456
18	4	356	8	238	220	10	2	0	18	3.498
IN	**36**	**3,714**	**26**	**894**	**2,488**	**776**	**103**	**15**		**36.169**
TOTAL	**72**	**7,313**	**55**	**1,823**	**5,178**	**1,366**	**161**	**21**		**71.619**

A putting savant of silent brutality

John Hopkins says the new Champion Golfer seems perfectly relaxed on the greens

Barely 12 hours before Cameron Smith putted out for victory on the 18th green of the Old Course, the ashes of Peter Thomson, Australia's greatest golfer, were sprinkled over the famous green. Thomson, who died in 2018, had won one of his five Opens at St Andrews in 1955. So when it came to the Claret Jug being claimed at this sacred venue once more, was there some karma at work? Aussie karma, perhaps?

We had seen the future, had we but known it. In Florida, in March, we were given a glimpse of the sort of golf Smith could produce when he won The Players Championship with a final round of 66, his lowest of the week by three strokes. Most significantly, in view of what he did at St Andrews four months later, he single-putted 13 of the last 18 greens on the Stadium Course at the Tournament Players Club. Cameron Smith, you see, putts as well as anyone.

So we shouldn't be surprised at the way he manhandled the Old Course with such silent brutality. Running off five successive birdies from the turn on Sunday was a knockout blow to his rivals. Some golfers back into victory when others collapse around them. Smith seems to do the opposite. He races past his rivals to victory, shoulder-charging them out of the way.

To say Smith, 28, is unobtrusive might be an exaggeration. Were it not for the thatch of hair that hangs from the back of his head like a safety curtain at a theatre, he would scarcely be noticeable at all. Quietly-spoken and modest, Smith is at the opposite end of the spectrum from his countryman, Greg Norman, the last Australian to win The Open in 1993, a month before Smith was born.

His is not the beefy power game of a Brooks Koepka or a Bryson DeChambeau, though he is long enough and can cause his irons to whistle through the air with the best of them. Coming up through the ranks in Australia, he was first their Amateur champion, then twice their PGA champion. He played a year on the Asian Tour before quickly establishing himself on the PGA Tour. He is both worldly wise and competitively hardened.

In addition, he appears to have a near supernatural relationship with his putter that is reminiscent of Ben Crenshaw, one of the greatest of all putters. Just as Seve Ballesteros looked born to address a golf ball, so comfortably did he take up the address position, and Crenshaw appeared completely at ease when softly holding a putter, so Smith seems perfectly relaxed on a putting green.

His body does not portray any of the anguish his mind might be enduring any more than Crenshaw's did in years gone by. There are times when Smith makes you think his ball just wouldn't dare to go anywhere but the hole, just as there were with Crenshaw.

Smith may be a putting savant, one to whom it comes easy. In an essay on putting Bernard Darwin, the great golf writer, talked about how amateurs and some professionals were unable to see a line to the hole "... or else half a hundred divergent lines all leading away from it. The green looks like a trackless waste of wild, barren country, dotted here and there with rocks and boulders. When we are on the edge of the green we seem to discern some sort of rough bridle-road; but as we approach the hole, it turns out to have been an illusion. A mere will-o'-the-wisp to deceive poor wayfarers."

Darwin continued that the greatest putters (and Smith is certainly one of those) see the target line as "...a light green avenue between dark green sidewalks, sometimes straight as an arrow, sometimes taking a graceful curve, but always leading straight to the goal so there is nothing to do but to start the ball rolling along it." That is how Smith putted in Florida in March and Scotland in July. Did we really think on that Sunday afternoon that Smith would not get his first putt deftly round the side of the Road Hole bunker without misadventure, and with just enough speed to crest a hill yet not so much it would race far past the flagstick? Did we really think he would not then stroke his second putt into the hole?

It was good to hear that while you can take the Australian out of Australia you can't take the irreverence and sense of fun of the stereotypical Australian out of the Australian. Smith posted photos of the celebrations after his victory, several countrymen of his with drinks in hand and he with his gold medal pinned to his chest. It was reassuring to know too, that in Jacksonville, Florida, where he lives with Shanel Naoum, his girlfriend, Smith has his collection of boats, cars and other boys' toys and that the weekend following his triumph in Scotland he was taking part in a fishing competition near his home. He may be quiet, but that doesn't mean he doesn't have a sense of how to enjoy himself.

EVERYTHING HAS LED TO THIS

Did we really think Smith would not stroke his second putt into the hole on the 17th?

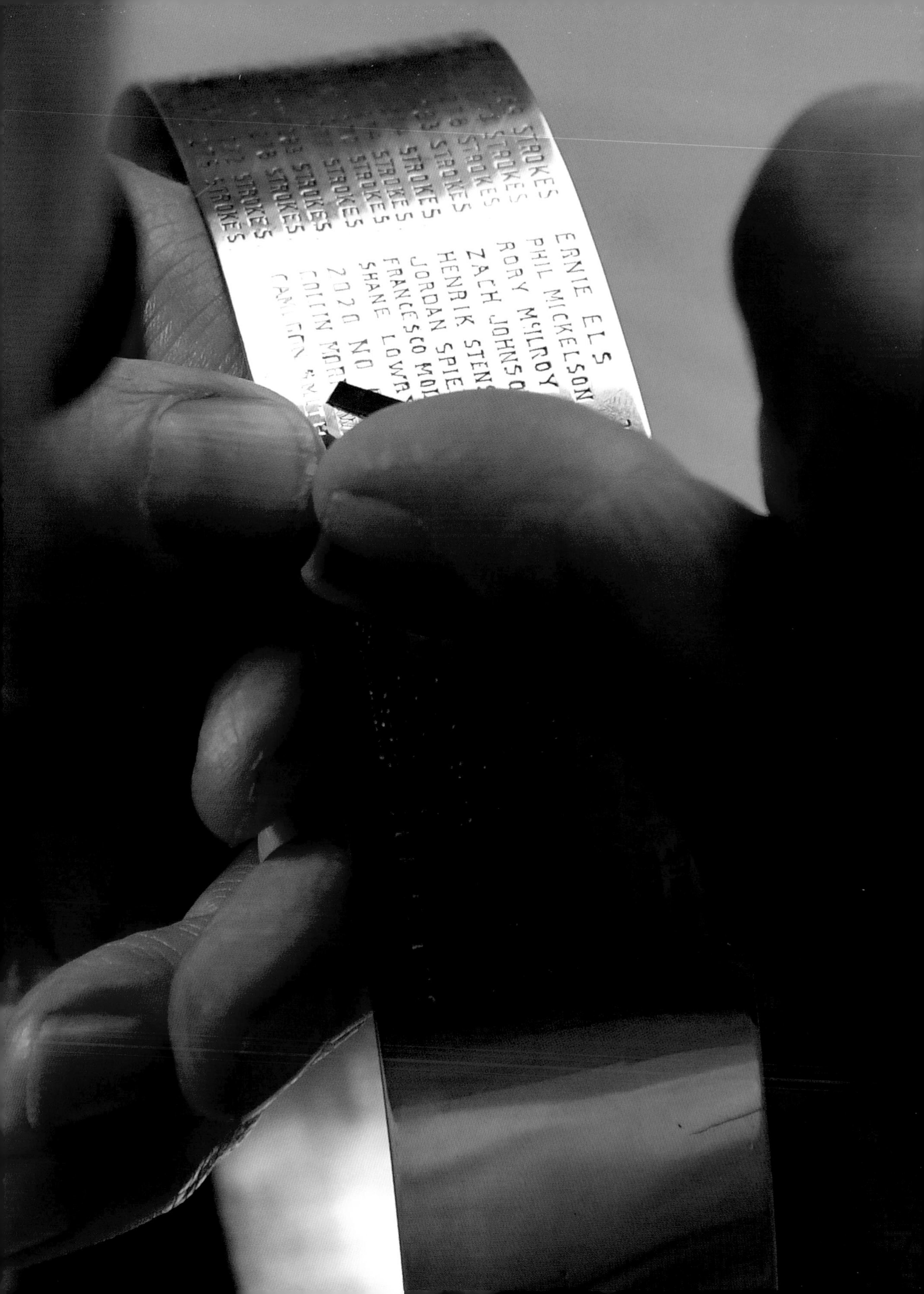

STROKES ERNIE ELS
STROKES PHIL MICKELSON
STROKES RORY McILROY
STROKES ZACH JOHNSON
STROKES HENRIK STENSON
STROKES JORDAN SPIE
STROKES FRANCESCO MO
STROKES SHANE LOWR
STROKES 2020 NO
STROKES COLLIN MOR
STROKES CAMERON SMITH

THE 150TH OPEN
COMPLETE SCORES

Old Course, St Andrews, Fife   14-17 July 2022

HOLE			1	2	3	4	5	6	7	8	9	10	11	12	13	14	15	16	17	18		
PAR	POS		4	4	4	5	4	4	3	4	4	3	4	3	4	5	4	4	4	4		TOTAL
Cameron Smith	T3	Rd1	4	3	4	4	4	4	3	3	4	3	4	3	4	5	4	4	4	3	67	
Australia	1	Rd2	3	3	3	4	5	4	3	2	4	3	3	4	4	3	4	4	4	4	64	
$2,500,000	T3	Rd3	5	4	4	4	5	4	4	3	3	4	3	4	6	4	4	4	4	4	73	
	1	Rd4	4	3	4	4	4	4	4	3	4	3	2	3	3	4	4	4	4	3	64	-20 **268**
Cameron Young	1	Rd1	4	3	3	4	4	3	4	3	3	4	2	3	4	5	4	4	4	3	64	
USA	2	Rd2	4	5	4	3	4	4	4	3	3	4	3	4	4	4	5	4	4	3	69	
$1,455,000	T3	Rd3	4	4	4	4	4	4	5	3	3	3	3	3	5	4	4	6	4	4	71	
	2	Rd4	5	4	3	3	4	4	3	3	5	3	3	4	3	4	4	4	4	2	65	-19 **269**
Rory McIlroy	2	Rd1	3	4	4	4	4	3	3	3	4	4	2	3	5	4	4	4	4	3	66	
Northern Ireland	T3	Rd2	4	4	4	4	4	4	3	4	4	3	2	3	4	5	5	4	3	4	68	
$933,000	T1	Rd3	4	4	4	4	4	3	4	3	3	2	3	4	4	4	4	4	5	3	66	
	3	Rd4	4	4	4	4	4	4	4	3	4	3	3	4	4	5	4	4	4	4	70	-18 **270**
Tommy Fleetwood	T55	Rd1	4	4	4	4	4	4	4	4	4	4	3	3	6	5	4	4	4	3	72	
England	T36	Rd2	4	5	4	4	4	4	4	3	3	3	3	4	4	4	4	3	5	4	69	
$654,000	T8	Rd3	3	3	4	4	4	3	4	3	4	4	4	4	4	3	4	4	4	3	66	
	T4	Rd4	3	4	4	4	4	4	3	3	4	4	3	4	4	4	4	4	4	3	67	-14 **274**
Viktor Hovland	T5	Rd1	3	4	3	5	5	4	4	3	3	4	3	4	5	5	4	3	3	3	68	
Norway	T3	Rd2	4	4	4	3	4	4	3	3	4	4	3	4	5	4	2	4	4	3	66	
$654,000	T1	Rd3	4	4	3	4	3	4	3	4	3	4	3	4	5	4	4	4	4	3	66	
	T4	Rd4	4	4	4	5	5	4	4	3	4	4	3	3	5	5	4	5	4	4	74	-14 **274**
Brian Harman	T77	Rd1	3	5	4	4	7	4	3	3	4	4	3	5	4	4	4	4	4	4	73	
USA	T36	Rd2	4	4	4	5	5	4	4	3	3	3	3	4	4	5	4	3	4	3	68	
$469,500	T13	Rd3	3	4	4	4	4	3	4	4	4	3	3	4	4	5	4	4	4	3	68	
	T6	Rd4	4	4	3	3	5	4	3	3	3	4	3	5	4	5	3	3	4	3	66	-13 **275**
Dustin Johnson	T5	Rd1	3	4	4	5	5	4	3	4	4	2	3	4	4	5	4	4	3	3	68	
USA	5	Rd2	5	4	3	4	5	4	4	3	3	3	3	4	4	4	4	3	4	3	67	
$469,500	7	Rd3	4	3	3	5	5	4	4	3	3	3	3	4	5	6	4	5	4	3	71	
	T6	Rd4	4	3	4	4	4	4	3	4	4	2	4	4	5	3	4	5	4	4	69	-13 **275**
Bryson DeChambeau	T13	Rd1	4	5	4	4	4	3	3	3	4	4	3	3	4	5	4	5	4	3	69	
USA	T55	Rd2	4	4	4	4	6	4	4	4	4	3	3	4	4	4	4	5	5	4	74	
$325,667	T18	Rd3	4	4	3	4	5	3	4	3	2	4	3	3	3	5	4	6	4	3	67	
	T8	Rd4	4	4	4	4	5	4	3	3	4	3	3	3	5	4	4	3	3	3	66	-12 **276**

(A) Denotes amateur

HOLE			1	2	3	4	5	6	7	8	9	10	11	12	13	14	15	16	17	18	
PAR	POS		4	4	4	4	5	4	4	3	4	4	3	4	4	5	4	4	4	4	TOTAL
Patrick Cantlay	T27	Rd1	4	4	5	4	5	4	3	3	4	3	3	4	4	4	5	4	4	3	70
USA	T8	Rd2	4	3	3	4	4	4	3	3	3	4	3	4	4	4	4	4	5	4	67
$325,667	T11	Rd3	4	4	3	4	4	3	4	3	3	4	3	5	4	5	4	6	4	4	71
	T8	Rd4	4	5	3	4	3	4	5	3	5	4	2	3	5	4	4	3	4	3	68 -12 **276**
Jordan Spieth	T35	Rd1	4	3	4	4	5	3	4	3	4	5	3	3	5	5	4	4	5	3	71
USA	T25	Rd2	4	3	4	4	4	4	3	3	3	4	3	4	5	4	4	4	5	4	69
$325,667	T11	Rd3	4	4	3	4	5	4	3	3	3	4	4	3	3	5	4	4	5	3	68
	T8	Rd4	4	3	3	4	4	4	3	4	4	3	3	4	4	6	3	4	4	4	68 -12 **276**
Sadom Kaewkanjana	T35	Rd1	4	4	4	4	5	6	4	3	3	4	5	3	4	4	4	4	3	3	71
Thailand	T12	Rd2	4	4	4	4	4	4	4	3	3	4	3	4	4	4	4	3	4	3	67
$231,000	T35	Rd3	4	5	4	4	5	4	4	3	4	4	3	6	4	5	4	4	4	3	74
	T11	Rd4	4	3	4	4	3	4	4	3	3	4	2	4	4	4	4	3	5	3	65 -11 **277**
Abraham Ancer	T35	Rd1	4	4	3	4	6	4	3	4	3	4	3	4	5	4	5	4	4	3	71
Mexico	T18	Rd2	4	4	4	3	4	4	4	3	4	4	2	4	4	4	4	4	4	4	68
$231,000	T35	Rd3	4	4	4	5	4	5	4	3	3	4	3	4	4	5	5	4	4	5	73
	T11	Rd4	4	4	4	4	5	3	3	2	4	3	3	4	4	5	3	3	4	3	65 -11 **277**
Dean Burmester	T35	Rd1	4	4	3	4	5	4	4	4	3	3	3	3	4	5	5	4	5	4	71
South Africa	T66	Rd2	3	4	4	4	5	3	4	3	5	5	3	4	5	5	5	3	5	3	73
$231,000	T24	Rd3	3	5	4	4	4	3	3	2	3	4	3	4	4	5	4	3	5	4	67
	T11	Rd4	4	4	3	4	3	4	4	2	4	3	3	4	3	5	3	4	5	4	66 -11 **277**
Tyrrell Hatton	T27	Rd1	4	4	4	4	5	4	5	3	3	4	3	5	3	4	4	4	4	3	70
England	T6	Rd2	4	4	4	4	5	3	3	3	3	3	3	4	4	4	4	4	4	3	66
$231,000	T13	Rd3	4	5	4	4	4	5	3	4	3	5	4	3	4	4	4	4	4	3	73
	T11	Rd4	4	3	3	4	4	3	4	4	4	4	3	4	4	5	4	3	5	3	68 -11 **277**
Lucas Herbert	T27	Rd1	4	3	4	3	5	5	4	3	3	4	3	4	4	5	4	4	4	4	70
Australia	T12	Rd2	4	3	4	4	4	4	4	3	3	3	4	4	4	5	4	4	4	3	68
$165,583	T24	Rd3	3	4	3	5	5	4	4	3	4	5	3	4	4	4	4	4	7	3	73
	T15	Rd4	4	5	3	4	4	3	4	3	3	4	3	4	4	4	3	4	4	4	67 -10 **278**
Xander Schauffele	T13	Rd1	5	4	3	4	4	4	3	3	4	3	3	4	4	4	4	4	5	4	69
USA	T18	Rd2	4	4	3	4	4	4	4	3	5	3	3	5	4	4	4	4	5	3	70
$165,583	T24	Rd3	4	4	4	4	5	3	3	3	3	4	3	6	6	4	4	4	5	2	72
	T15	Rd4	3	3	3	4	5	5	3	3	4	4	3	4	3	4	4	4	5	4	67 -10 **278**
Anthony Quayle	T101	Rd1	3	4	4	5	5	5	5	4	3	4	3	4	4	5	5	4	4	3	74
Australia	T55	Rd2	3	5	4	4	4	4	4	3	4	3	3	3	4	4	4	4	5	4	69
$165,583	T24	Rd3	3	4	4	4	4	4	5	3	3	3	5	3	4	3	4	6	5	3	68
	T15	Rd4	4	4	3	4	4	5	4	2	4	3	3	3	4	4	4	4	4	4	67 -10 **278**
Francesco Molinari	T77	Rd1	4	4	4	4	5	4	4	3	3	4	3	4	5	5	4	5	4	4	73
Italy	T66	Rd2	4	4	4	4	4	4	3	3	5	4	3	3	4	4	4	5	4	5	71
$165,583	T18	Rd3	3	4	3	3	5	4	4	3	3	3	4	4	4	4	4	3	4	4	66
	T15	Rd4	4	4	3	4	4	4	3	3	3	3	3	4	4	4	4	4	5	4	68 -10 **278**
Adam Scott	T55	Rd1	4	5	4	6	5	5	4	3	3	4	2	3	4	5	4	4	4	3	72
Australia	T8	Rd2	4	4	3	4	4	4	4	3	3	3	2	4	4	4	4	4	4	3	65
$165,583	T8	Rd3	4	4	4	5	4	4	5	4	3	3	3	4	3	5	4	3	5	3	70
	T15	Rd4	4	3	4	4	4	4	3	3	4	3	3	6	4	5	4	4	5	4	71 -10 **278**
Si Woo Kim	T13	Rd1	3	6	3	4	4	5	4	3	4	4	2	3	4	4	4	4	4	4	69
Korea	T12	Rd2	3	4	4	4	5	4	4	3	4	3	3	4	4	5	3	4	5	3	69
$165,583	T5	Rd3	4	4	4	4	4	4	3	3	4	3	3	4	4	4	3	5	4	3	67
	T15	Rd4	4	4	4	4	5	4	3	4	5	4	3	4	5	4	5	3	4	4	73 -10 **278**

	POS		1	2	3	4	5	6	7	8	9	10	11	12	13	14	15	16	17	18		TOTAL
PAR	POS		4	4	4	4	5	4	4	3	4	4	3	4	5	4	4	4	4	4		TOTAL
Billy Horschel	T77	Rd1	3	4	4	4	4	4	3	3	4	5	3	5	5	5	4	5	5	3	73	
USA	T46	Rd2	4	4	4	4	4	4	4	3	3	3	3	4	4	5	5	4	4	3	69	
$120,286	T35	Rd3	4	4	3	4	5	4	4	3	3	4	2	4	4	6	4	4	4	4	70	
	T21	Rd4	4	3	3	4	6	5	4	3	3	3	3	3	4	5	3	3	4	4	67	-9 **279**
Min Woo Lee	T13	Rd1	4	4	6	3	5	4	4	2	3	4	3	3	4	3	4	4	5	4	69	
Australia	T12	Rd2	3	4	4	5	5	4	4	3	4	3	3	2	5	4	5	3	5	3	69	
$120,286	T24	Rd3	4	5	5	3	4	4	4	3	3	4	4	4	4	5	4	5	4	4	73	
	T21	Rd4	4	4	3	4	4	4	4	3	3	4	3	4	6	4	3	4	4	3	68	-9 **279**
Trey Mullinax	T35	Rd1	4	4	4	4	4	4	5	3	3	3	3	5	4	4	4	4	5	4	71	
USA	T66	Rd2	4	4	4	4	4	4	4	3	4	5	3	5	4	5	3	4	5	4	73	
$120,286	T18	Rd3	4	3	3	4	4	4	3	3	4	4	3	3	4	4	4	4	5	3	66	
	T21	Rd4	3	4	4	3	5	4	4	3	3	3	3	5	3	5	4	4	6	3	69	-9 **279**
Shane Lowry	T55	Rd1	4	6	4	5	4	4	4	3	3	3	3	4	5	4	4	4	4	4	72	
Republic of Ireland	T25	Rd2	4	4	4	4	4	4	4	3	3	3	3	3	4	5	4	6	3	3	68	
$120,286	T13	Rd3	4	4	3	5	5	3	4	3	2	2	3	5	4	5	5	4	5	3	69	
	T21	Rd4	4	4	3	4	5	4	4	3	4	3	3	4	4	5	4	5	4	3	70	-9 **279**
Kevin Kisner	T101	Rd1	3	5	4	5	5	4	4	3	4	4	4	3	4	5	5	4	4	4	74	
USA	T66	Rd2	4	5	4	4	4	3	4	4	4	4	2	5	4	4	5	3	4	3	70	
$120,286	T13	Rd3	3	3	3	4	4	3	4	2	4	3	3	5	4	4	4	3	5	4	65	
	T21	Rd4	4	4	4	3	4	3	4	3	3	4	3	4	5	5	4	5	4	4	70	-9 **279**
Matt Fitzpatrick	T55	Rd1	4	4	4	5	5	4	4	3	4	3	4	3	4	5	4	5	4	3	72	
England	T12	Rd2	4	3	4	3	5	5	3	3	3	4	3	3	4	5	3	3	4	4	66	
$120,286	T8	Rd3	4	4	4	5	5	4	4	3	3	3	2	4	4	4	4	4	5	3	69	
	T21	Rd4	4	4	4	4	4	4	4	3	4	3	3	4	4	5	5	5	5	3	72	-9 **279**
Scottie Scheffler	T5	Rd1	4	4	3	3	4	4	4	3	3	4	3	4	5	4	4	4	4	4	68	
USA	T6	Rd2	5	4	4	4	5	4	3	3	4	3	2	3	4	5	4	4	4	3	68	
$120,286	T5	Rd3	4	4	3	4	4	4	4	3	4	3	2	5	4	5	4	4	5	3	69	
	T21	Rd4	4	4	4	4	6	5	4	3	5	3	3	4	4	5	4	5	4	3	74	-9 **279**
Tony Finau	T77	Rd1	4	4	4	4	6	4	4	4	3	3	3	3	5	5	5	4	5	3	73	
USA	T66	Rd2	3	6	4	4	5	4	4	3	3	4	2	3	4	5	4	5	5	3	71	
$90,917	T55	Rd3	4	5	4	4	5	3	4	3	2	4	2	4	4	5	4	5	5	3	70	
	T28	Rd4	4	4	5	4	4	4	3	3	3	3	3	3	4	4	4	3	5	3	66	-8 **280**
Corey Conners	T35	Rd1	4	4	3	5	4	4	4	3	3	4	3	4	5	4	4	5	5	3	71	
Canada	T46	Rd2	5	3	4	5	6	4	3	3	4	3	3	4	4	5	4	3	4	4	71	
$90,917	T48	Rd3	4	4	3	4	4	4	4	3	3	5	3	4	4	5	4	5	5	3	71	
	T28	Rd4	4	4	3	4	4	4	4	4	3	4	3	3	4	4	3	4	5	3	67	-8 **280**
Harold Varner III	T77	Rd1	4	3	4	5	5	5	4	4	4	4	4	3	4	4	4	5	4	3	73	
USA	T25	Rd2	4	3	4	4	4	4	3	3	3	4	3	3	4	4	4	5	4	4	67	
$90,917	T35	Rd3	3	4	4	5	4	4	5	3	4	3	3	4	4	5	4	4	6	3	72	
	T28	Rd4	3	4	3	4	4	5	4	3	3	3	3	5	4	3	5	4	5	3	68	-8 **280**
Will Zalatoris	T77	Rd1	4	5	4	4	5	4	4	4	3	4	3	4	5	4	4	4	4	4	73	
USA	T25	Rd2	5	4	3	4	4	4	4	2	3	3	3	3	4	6	4	4	4	3	67	
$90,917	T24	Rd3	3	4	5	4	4	3	4	3	3	4	3	4	4	5	5	5	5	3	71	
	T28	Rd4	5	3	4	4	5	3	4	2	3	4	3	3	4	5	4	3	6	4	69	-8 **280**
Dylan Frittelli	T27	Rd1	3	4	3	3	5	5	5	2	3	4	3	4	4	6	4	4	5	3	70	
South Africa	T36	Rd2	6	3	3	5	4	4	4	3	4	4	3	3	4	4	5	4	4	4	71	
$90,917	T18	Rd3	4	4	4	4	4	4	4	4	2	5	2	5	4	4	4	4	5	2	69	
	T28	Rd4	4	3	4	4	4	4	4	3	3	4	3	3	5	6	4	4	5	3	70	-8 **280**

HOLE			1	2	3	4	5	6	7	8	9	10	11	12	13	14	15	16	17	18			
PAR	POS		4	4	4	4	5	4	4	3	4	4	3	4	4	5	4	4	4	4			TOTAL
Thomas Pieters	T119	Rd1	4	5	4	5	5	4	5	3	4	4	3	4	4	5	4	4	4	4	75		
Belgium	T46	Rd2	3	4	4	4	4	3	3	3	3	4	3	4	4	4	4	5	4	4	67		
$90,917	T13	Rd3	4	5	3	4	4	4	3	3	2	3	3	4	3	4	5	5	5	3	67		
	T28	**Rd4**	4	5	3	3	5	4	3	3	3	4	4	4	4	6	4	4	5	3	71	-8	**280**
Thomas Detry	T27	Rd1	4	3	4	5	4	3	4	4	4	4	4	4	4	4	3	4	4	4	70		
Belgium	T18	Rd2	4	3	4	6	5	3	3	3	4	4	4	4	4	5	3	3	4	3	69		
$68,906	T48	Rd3	4	4	4	4	4	3	5	3	4	4	3	4	5	4	5	5	5	4	74		
	T34	**Rd4**	4	6	3	5	4	3	4	3	3	3	3	4	5	4	3	4	5	2	68	-7	**281**
Robert MacIntyre	T27	Rd1	4	3	3	4	5	5	4	2	4	3	3	3	6	5	4	4	5	3	70		
Scotland	T66	Rd2	4	5	4	5	4	4	4	3	4	4	3	4	5	4	5	4	4	4	74		
$68,906	T48	Rd3	4	5	3	4	5	4	3	3	4	3	3	4	5	4	4	3	4	4	69		
	T34	**Rd4**	6	4	3	4	3	4	3	4	4	4	3	2	4	4	4	4	4	4	68	-7	**281**
Talor Gooch	T5	Rd1	3	3	4	4	4	4	5	4	3	4	3	3	4	6	4	4	3	3	68		
USA	T8	Rd2	3	4	3	4	5	4	4	3	4	4	3	4	4	4	5	4	3	4	69		
$68,906	T35	Rd3	4	4	3	5	5	4	4	3	3	4	2	4	4	7	5	5	5	4	75		
	T34	**Rd4**	4	4	4	4	4	4	3	3	4	4	3	4	3	5	4	5	4	3	69	-7	**281**
Lee Westwood	T5	Rd1	4	6	4	3	4	4	4	3	3	3	3	4	4	4	3	4	5	3	68		
England	T18	Rd2	3	5	4	5	5	4	4	3	4	4	2	4	4	5	4	4	3	4	71		
$68,906	T35	Rd3	4	5	4	4	5	4	5	3	3	4	3	5	5	5	4	3	4	3	73		
	T34	**Rd4**	5	5	3	4	4	3	3	3	4	4	3	4	4	4	4	3	6	3	69	-7	**281**
Sahith Theegala	T13	Rd1	3	4	4	5	4	4	3	3	3	3	4	3	4	5	5	4	4	4	69		
USA	T8	Rd2	5	4	3	4	4	4	4	4	2	4	3	3	4	4	4	4	4	4	68		
$68,906	T24	Rd3	4	4	4	5	5	4	4	4	4	4	3	4	4	4	5	4	4	4	74		
	T34	**Rd4**	4	4	3	4	4	5	4	3	4	4	3	3	4	4	4	4	5	4	70	-7	**281**
Jon Rahm	T77	Rd1	4	4	3	4	5	3	4	4	4	4	3	4	5	5	5	4	4	4	73		
Spain	T25	Rd2	3	3	4	4	4	4	4	3	3	4	3	4	4	4	5	4	4	3	67		
$68,906	T24	Rd3	4	5	4	4	5	5	4	3	3	4	3	4	4	3	5	4	4	3	71		
	T34	**Rd4**	4	4	5	6	4	3	4	3	3	4	3	4	4	4	4	4	4	3	70	-7	**281**
Victor Perez	T35	Rd1	4	4	4	4	4	4	4	3	3	4	3	3	5	5	5	4	4	4	71		
France	T25	Rd2	4	5	4	4	4	4	4	4	4	3	3	3	3	4	4	5	4	3	69		
$68,906	T24	Rd3	4	4	4	4	4	4	4	3	3	3	4	5	4	5	4	4	5	3	71		
	T34	**Rd4**	5	4	4	4	4	4	4	3	4	4	3	3	4	4	4	4	4	4	70	-7	**281**
Aaron Wise	T55	Rd1	4	4	4	5	4	4	5	3	3	4	4	3	4	5	4	3	5	4	72		
USA	T18	Rd2	3	4	4	4	4	3	4	4	4	3	4	3	4	5	3	4	4	3	67		
$68,906	T18	Rd3	4	6	3	4	5	4	4	3	3	3	3	3	5	4	4	4	5	4	71		
	T34	**Rd4**	4	4	3	4	5	3	4	3	4	4	3	4	5	4	5	5	4	3	71	-7	**281**
Sam Burns	T55	Rd1	4	4	4	4	4	4	4	4	4	5	3	3	5	5	5	3	4	3	72		
USA	T36	Rd2	3	5	3	3	4	4	3	3	4	4	3	3	4	4	5	4	6	4	69		
$51,000	T77	Rd3	3	4	3	4	4	5	4	3	3	5	4	5	6	5	5	6	4	4	77		
	T42	**Rd4**	4	4	4	3	4	4	3	3	4	3	3	4	4	5	3	3	3	3	64	-6	**282**
Jason Kokrak	T55	Rd1	3	4	5	4	5	4	4	3	4	4	4	4	5	6	3	3	4	3	72		
USA	T46	Rd2	4	4	3	4	4	4	4	3	4	3	4	4	4	6	3	5	4	3	70		
$51,000	T55	Rd3	4	5	4	4	5	4	5	3	2	3	4	4	5	4	5	5	4	2	72		
	T42	**Rd4**	4	4	3	4	4	4	4	3	3	4	4	3	4	5	4	3	5	3	68	-6	**282**
Thriston Lawrence	T13	Rd1	3	5	3	4	4	4	4	4	3	3	4	3	4	4	5	4	3	5	69		
South Africa	T25	Rd2	4	4	5	4	5	3	5	3	3	5	3	3	4	4	4	5	4	3	71		
$51,000	T48	Rd3	4	4	4	4	4	5	4	3	4	5	3	4	4	4	4	4	5	4	73		
	T42	**Rd4**	4	4	4	4	4	4	5	2	3	4	3	4	4	4	5	4	4	3	69	-6	**282**

HOLE			1	2	3	4	5	6	7	8	9	10	11	12	13	14	15	16	17	18		TOTAL
PAR	POS		4	4	4	4	5	4	4	3	4	4	3	4	4	5	4	4	4	4		
Adrian Meronk	T119	Rd1	5	4	5	4	5	5	4	4	5	5	3	3	4	4	4	4	4	3	75	
Poland	T55	Rd2	4	4	4	4	4	4	4	3	4	4	3	3	3	5	4	4	4	3	68	
$51,000	T48	Rd3	4	4	3	4	5	3	3	3	4	4	3	4	5	5	4	3	5	4	70	
	T42	Rd4	4	4	4	4	4	4	4	3	3	4	4	4	3	4	4	4	4	4	69	-6 **282**
Chris Kirk	T119	Rd1	4	4	5	4	5	5	4	3	4	4	3	3	5	6	4	4	4	4	75	
USA	T55	Rd2	4	4	4	4	3	4	4	2	3	3	3	4	4	5	5	4	4	4	68	
$51,000	T35	Rd3	3	4	3	4	5	3	4	3	3	4	3	5	4	4	4	4	5	4	69	
	T42	Rd4	4	3	4	4	4	4	3	2	4	4	5	3	4	6	4	4	4	4	70	-6 **282**
Garrick Higgo	T55	Rd1	4	4	4	5	5	5	4	2	3	4	4	4	4	5	3	4	4	4	72	
South Africa	T36	Rd2	3	3	3	3	5	4	4	3	4	4	2	4	4	5	4	5	5	4	69	
$40,600	T75	Rd3	4	5	4	4	3	4	5	3	4	5	4	5	4	5	4	5	5	3	76	
	T47	Rd4	4	4	4	5	4	4	3	3	2	4	3	3	4	5	3	4	3	4	66	-5 **283**
Patrick Reed	T55	Rd1	4	4	3	5	5	4	3	3	4	4	4	3	5	5	4	3	5	4	72	
USA	T25	Rd2	3	4	4	4	4	3	4	3	4	3	3	4	4	4	5	4	4	4	68	
$40,600	T69	Rd3	4	4	4	4	6	4	4	3	4	5	3	5	4	5	3	6	5	3	76	
	T47	Rd4	4	4	4	4	5	3	3	3	4	3	3	4	5	4	4	3	4		67	-5 **283**
Jordan Smith	T77	Rd1	5	4	4	5	3	4	4	4	4	4	3	4	4	4	5	4	4	4	73	
England	T66	Rd2	5	3	4	4	4	4	4	3	3	4	3	4	4	6	5	3	4	4	71	
$40,600	T69	Rd3	3	4	4	5	4	4	5	3	5	4	2	4	5	4	4	4	4	4	72	
	T47	Rd4	4	4	3	4	4	4	5	3	3	3	3	5	3	3	4	3	6	3	67	-5 **283**
Yuto Katsuragawa	T35	Rd1	3	4	4	5	6	4	3	3	4	4	3	3	4	5	4	5	4	3	71	
Japan	T18	Rd2	5	3	4	4	4	4	4	3	3	3	3	4	4	5	4	4	4	3	68	
$40,600	T55	Rd3	4	4	4	4	7	5	4	3	4	4	3	4	5	4	4	4	5	3	75	
	T47	Rd4	4	4	3	6	4	3	3	3	4	4	3	4	4	4	4	4	4	4	69	-5 **283**
Joohyung Kim	T13	Rd1	4	4	3	4	4	4	3	3	3	4	3	4	4	5	3	5	5	4	69	
Korea	T25	Rd2	4	3	4	4	6	4	4	3	5	3	3	4	4	4	4	4	5	3	71	
$40,600	T35	Rd3	4	3	4	5	5	4	4	3	5	5	3	4	4	4	4	5	4	4	72	
	T47	Rd4	4	4	4	4	5	3	4	3	5	5	3	4	4	5	4	4	5	3	71	-5 **283**
Filippo Celli[A]	T101	Rd1	4	4	4	5	4	4	4	3	4	5	4	3	4	4	5	4	6	3	74	
Italy	T36	Rd2	4	4	4	4	4	4	4	3	3	4	2	4	4	4	4	4	4	3	67	
	T35	Rd3	4	4	4	4	4	4	4	3	3	4	4	4	4	6	3	4	5	3	71	
	T47	Rd4	4	5	5	4	4	3	5	3	3	4	4	4	4	3	4	4	5	3	71	-5 **283**
Joaquin Niemann	T13	Rd1	3	4	4	4	5	5	4	3	4	3	3	3	4	5	4	3	4	4	69	
Chile	T55	Rd2	4	6	4	4	4	4	4	4	3	4	3	5	4	4	4	5	4	4	74	
$35,656	T69	Rd3	4	4	4	4	4	4	4	3	3	3	3	4	4	6	4	6	5	4	73	
	T53	Rd4	4	4	4	4	4	3	4	3	5	3	3	3	4	4	4	4	5	3	68	-4 **284**
Danny Willett	T13	Rd1	4	3	4	5	4	4	3	3	4	4	3	3	6	4	4	4	5	2	69	
England	T46	Rd2	4	4	4	4	4	5	4	4	4	3	3	4	4	6	4	3	5	4	73	
$35,656	T64	Rd3	4	4	4	4	4	4	3	4	4	3	3	4	5	8	4	4	4	3	73	
	T53	Rd4	3	4	5	5	4	3	4	3	3	4	3	4	5	4	4	3	4	4	69	-4 **284**
Robert Dinwiddie	T3	Rd1	3	4	4	4	4	3	4	3	4	3	3	4	4	5	3	5	4	3	67	
England	T66	Rd2	4	5	4	5	5	4	3	4	4	5	3	4	5	6	4	4	4	4	77	
$35,656	T64	Rd3	4	5	5	4	4	4	4	3	3	4	3	4	3	5	4	4	5	3	71	
	T53	Rd4	5	4	3	4	4	4	4	3	3	4	3	4	4	4	4	3	5	4	69	-4 **284**
Lars Van Meijel	T101	Rd1	4	5	4	4	5	4	4	3	5	4	4	4	4	5	4	4	5	3	74	
Netherlands	T66	Rd2	4	4	4	4	5	4	4	3	3	4	3	3	4	5	5	4	4	3	70	
$35,656	T64	Rd3	4	4	3	5	4	4	4	3	4	3	3	4	4	4	4	5	5	4	71	
	T53	Rd4	4	5	4	4	3	4	4	2	4	4	3	4	5	4	4	3	5	3	69	-4 **284**

HOLE		1	2	3	4	5	6	7	8	9	10	11	12	13	14	15	16	17	18	
PAR	POS	4	4	4	4	5	4	4	3	4	4	3	4	4	5	4	4	4	4	**TOTAL**
Justin Thomas	T55 Rd1	4	4	4	4	4	4	4	3	3	4	3	4	4	5	4	4	6	4	72
USA	T46 Rd2	5	4	4	4	3	4	4	4	4	3	3	3	4	4	5	4	4	4	70
$35,656	T55 Rd3	4	3	4	5	5	4	4	3	4	5	4	5	4	5	3	4	3	3	72
	T53 Rd4	5	3	4	5	3	3	4	2	4	4	3	4	4	7	4	3	5	3	70 -4 **284**
Paul Casey	T35 Rd1	4	4	3	4	4	3	4	2	4	4	4	4	4	5	5	4	5	4	71
England	T55 Rd2	4	3	4	4	4	3	4	3	4	4	3	5	5	4	4	5	6	3	72
$35,656	T55 Rd3	4	4	3	4	4	4	3	3	3	4	4	4	4	4	5	5	5	4	71
	T53 Rd4	4	4	3	3	4	5	4	3	4	4	3	4	4	4	3	5	6	3	70 -4 **284**
Jason Scrivener	T55 Rd1	4	5	4	5	5	4	4	3	3	4	3	3	5	5	4	3	4	4	72
Australia	T55 Rd2	4	4	4	4	4	5	4	3	3	5	3	4	4	4	4	4	5	3	71
$35,656	T55 Rd3	4	3	3	4	5	4	4	3	3	4	3	3	4	7	4	4	5	4	71
	T53 Rd4	4	5	4	4	5	4	4	3	3	3	3	3	4	5	4	4	4	4	70 -4 **284**
Brad Kennedy	T5 Rd1	3	4	3	4	4	3	4	4	5	3	2	5	5	4	4	4	4	3	68
Australia	T25 Rd2	4	4	5	4	4	5	3	3	4	3	3	4	4	5	4	5	4	4	72
$35,656	T35 Rd3	4	4	5	5	5	4	3	3	3	4	3	4	5	5	4	4	4	3	72
	T53 Rd4	4	4	4	5	5	3	4	2	4	4	3	3	5	5	3	5	5	4	72 -4 **284**
Nicolai Højgaard	T77 Rd1	4	6	4	4	4	3	4	3	3	4	3	4	5	5	4	4	5	4	73
Denmark	T25 Rd2	4	3	4	4	4	4	4	2	3	4	3	4	4	5	3	4	5	3	67
$35,656	T24 Rd3	4	4	4	5	5	5	4	3	3	3	5	3	4	4	4	4	4	3	71
	T53 Rd4	4	4	4	4	4	4	4	3	4	3	4	4	3	6	4	6	4	4	73 -4 **284**
Cameron Tringale	T35 Rd1	3	4	3	4	5	3	4	3	4	4	4	4	4	5	5	4	4	4	71
USA	T46 Rd2	4	4	4	4	4	4	4	4	4	3	3	4	4	4	4	4	5	4	71
$33,625	T69 Rd3	3	5	4	4	4	5	3	3	3	4	3	4	5	5	4	4	6	5	74
	T62 Rd4	3	4	3	4	5	4	4	3	3	3	3	4	3	5	4	4	7	3	69 -3 **285**
Sebastián Muñoz	T77 Rd1	4	4	4	5	4	4	3	3	4	4	4	3	4	7	5	4	4	3	73
Colombia	T66 Rd2	5	4	4	4	5	4	4	2	4	4	3	3	4	4	5	4	4	4	71
$33,625	T64 Rd3	4	4	4	4	5	4	5	3	3	3	3	4	5	4	4	4	4	4	71
	T62 Rd4	4	4	3	5	5	3	4	3	3	4	3	4	3	6	4	4	4	4	70 -3 **285**
John Parry	T13 Rd1	3	5	4	5	4	4	3	4	4	3	3	5	3	4	4	3	4	4	69
England	T55 Rd2	4	4	3	4	5	5	4	3	5	3	3	4	5	6	4	4	4	4	74
$33,625	T48 Rd3	4	4	4	4	6	4	3	2	3	3	4	5	4	4	4	4	5	3	70
	T62 Rd4	4	4	4	4	4	4	4	3	4	4	3	4	4	4	4	6	4	4	72 -3 **285**
David Carey	T55 Rd1	3	4	5	5	5	3	4	4	3	4	3	4	4	5	4	4	5	3	72
Republic of Ireland	T18 Rd2	4	3	4	4	5	5	3	3	3	4	2	3	3	5	4	4	4	4	67
$33,625	T35 Rd3	5	4	3	4	4	5	4	3	3	4	4	4	4	4	4	5	6	3	73
	T62 Rd4	5	3	4	4	4	4	3	3	4	3	5	4	4	6	4	4	6	3	73 -3 **285**
Ian Poulter	T13 Rd1	4	4	4	4	5	3	4	3	2	4	3	4	4	6	4	4	4	3	69
England	T36 Rd2	3	5	3	4	5	4	4	3	3	5	4	3	4	5	4	5	4	4	72
$33,625	T24 Rd3	3	4	4	3	5	4	3	4	3	5	4	4	4	4	4	4	5	3	70
	T62 Rd4	4	4	4	4	5	4	3	2	4	4	4	5	4	5	4	4	6	4	74 -3 **285**
Russell Henley	T27 Rd1	4	4	4	5	5	4	4	2	4	4	4	3	4	4	4	4	4	3	70
USA	T46 Rd2	5	4	4	4	5	3	4	3	4	3	4	4	5	5	4	4	4	3	72
$33,625	T18 Rd3	3	4	4	4	4	4	3	3	3	4	3	4	4	5	5	4	4	3	68
	T62 Rd4	4	4	5	5	6	3	4	3	3	4	3	5	3	5	5	5	4	4	75 -3 **285**
Hideki Matsuyama	T35 Rd1	4	4	5	4	4	4	4	2	4	4	3	3	5	5	4	4	5	3	71
Japan	T55 Rd2	3	4	3	4	5	4	4	3	4	4	3	4	5	5	4	5	5	3	72
$32,525	80 Rd3	4	4	4	5	5	7	3	3	3	4	4	4	4	7	4	4	4	3	76
	T68 Rd4	4	4	3	4	4	3	4	3	4	3	3	3	5	4	4	4	5	3	67 -2 **286**

HOLE			1	2	3	4	5	6	7	8	9	10	11	12	13	14	15	16	17	18			TOTAL
PAR		POS	4	4	4	4	5	4	4	3	4	4	3	4	4	5	4	4	4	4			TOTAL
Sergio Garcia	T119	Rd1	4	4	4	5	5	4	4	3	4	4	3	3	4	5	5	4	7	3	75		
Spain	T36	Rd2	4	4	4	4	4	4	3	3	2	4	2	3	4	4	4	4	5	4	66		
$32,525	T48	Rd3	4	3	3	4	7	4	4	4	3	4	3	3	4	5	5	3	4	5	72		
	T68	Rd4	4	3	4	4	4	4	4	4	5	4	3	5	4	6	3	3	6	3	73	-2	**286**
Christiaan Bezuidenhout	T77	Rd1	3	4	3	5	4	5	4	3	3	4	3	5	6	6	5	4	3	3	73		
South Africa	T66	Rd2	4	5	4	4	5	4	4	2	3	4	3	4	4	4	4	5	5	3	71		
$32,525	T35	Rd3	3	4	4	4	4	3	4	3	3	3	3	4	5	5	4	4	4	4	68		
	T68	Rd4	4	5	4	4	6	4	4	3	4	3	3	4	4	6	4	4	4	4	74	-2	**286**
Richard Mansell	T77	Rd1	4	4	3	4	5	5	5	4	3	4	4	3	5	4	5	4	4	3	73		
England	T66	Rd2	4	4	5	4	6	4	4	3	4	3	3	4	4	4	3	4	4	4	71		
$32,525	T35	Rd3	4	3	4	5	4	4	4	3	2	3	4	3	5	4	4	3	5	4	68		
	T68	Rd4	4	4	3	4	5	4	4	3	4	3	4	4	5	7	3	4	5	4	74	-2	**286**
David Law	T55	Rd1	4	4	4	5	6	4	4	3	4	4	3	3	4	4	4	3	5	4	72		
Scotland	T36	Rd2	4	4	4	5	4	4	4	3	4	4	3	4	3	4	4	4	4	3	69		
$32,013	T77	Rd3	4	4	4	6	5	6	4	3	3	4	3	4	5	4	5	4	5	3	77		
	T72	Rd4	3	4	3	4	4	4	5	3	5	3	3	4	5	5	3	4	4	3	69	-1	**287**
Kurt Kitayama	T5	Rd1	4	4	4	4	4	4	4	2	4	4	3	3	4	5	4	4	4	3	68		
USA	T36	Rd2	4	5	4	5	5	4	4	2	2	4	4	3	5	4	4	4	6	4	73		
$32,013	T55	Rd3	5	5	4	4	5	4	4	3	4	4	3	3	5	5	4	4	4	3	73		
	T72	Rd4	5	4	4	5	4	4	4	3	4	4	3	3	5	5	5	4	4	3	73	-1	**287**
Marcus Armitage	T35	Rd1	4	4	4	3	5	5	5	3	4	3	3	3	4	5	4	4	4	4	71		
England	T55	Rd2	4	4	4	4	4	3	4	3	3	4	3	5	4	6	5	4	5	3	72		
$31,763	T55	Rd3	3	4	5	4	4	4	4	2	3	4	4	5	4	4	4	4	5	3	71		
	T74	Rd4	4	4	5	5	5	4	4	3	4	4	3	4	4	5	4	4	4	4	74	E	**288**
Justin De Los Santos	T35	Rd1	4	5	4	3	5	4	4	3	4	4	4	2	4	5	4	4	5	3	71		
Philippines	T66	Rd2	4	5	4	4	6	4	3	3	4	4	3	4	5	4	4	4	4	4	73		
$31,763	T55	Rd3	3	6	4	4	5	4	3	3	4	4	3	3	4	4	4	4	4	4	70		
	T74	Rd4	4	4	4	4	5	4	4	3	5	3	3	4	4	8	4	4	4	3	74	E	**288**
Wyndham Clark	T35	Rd1	4	4	4	5	5	5	5	3	3	4	3	2	4	4	5	4	4	3	71		
USA	T66	Rd2	4	5	4	4	5	5	3	3	3	5	3	4	5	5	4	4	4	3	73		
$31,513	81	Rd3	4	4	4	5	4	3	5	3	3	4	3	3	5	7	5	6	5	3	76		
	T76	Rd4	4	4	4	5	5	4	4	3	3	4	2	3	3	5	4	4	5	3	69	+1	**289**
Adri Arnaus	T101	Rd1	4	4	3	4	5	5	4	3	4	4	4	5	4	5	4	4	4	4	74		
Spain	T66	Rd2	3	4	4	4	4	3	4	3	4	4	5	3	4	5	4	4	5	3	70		
$31,513	T75	Rd3	4	4	4	4	5	4	4	3	3	5	3	4	4	5	4	5	5	3	73		
	T76	Rd4	4	5	4	4	5	4	3	3	4	4	3	4	4	6	5	4	4	2	72	+1	**289**
Aaron Jarvis[A]	T119	Rd1	4	5	4	5	6	4	4	3	3	4	3	3	5	6	4	4	4	4	75		
Cayman Islands	T66	Rd2	4	4	4	4	5	4	3	2	3	4	3	4	4	4	4	4	5	4	69		
	T69	Rd3	4	3	4	4	5	4	3	3	4	4	5	4	5	4	4	4	5	3	72		
	T76	Rd4	4	4	4	5	6	4	4	3	4	4	3	3	4	6	4	3	4	4	73	+1	**289**
Laurie Canter	T55	Rd1	5	5	4	4	4	4	4	3	3	3	3	4	5	5	4	3	5	4	72		
England	T46	Rd2	6	4	4	4	6	3	3	2	3	3	3	5	4	4	4	4	4	4	70		
$31,325	T69	Rd3	4	4	5	4	4	4	3	4	3	4	3	5	4	6	4	5	4	4	74		
	T79	Rd4	4	5	4	6	5	4	3	3	4	4	3	4	4	5	4	4	5	3	74	+2	**290**
Barclay Brown[A]	T5	Rd1	4	4	4	4	5	4	3	3	3	5	3	3	4	4	4	4	3	4	68		
England	T12	Rd2	4	5	4	5	4	4	4	2	3	4	4	4	4	6	3	3	4	3	70		
	T64	Rd3	4	4	5	5	5	4	3	3	4	3	4	4	6	5	5	5	4		77		
	T79	Rd4	4	4	3	4	5	4	3	3	4	4	3	4	5	6	5	5	6	3	75	+2	**290**

HOLE			1	2	3	4	5	6	7	8	9	10	11	12	13	14	15	16	17	18			
PAR	POS		4	4	4	4	5	4	4	3	4	4	3	4	4	5	4	4	4	4	TOTAL		
Sam Bairstow[A]	T55	Rd1	4	4	4	5	5	4	5	3	2	5	5	3	3	5	4	4	4	3	72		
England	T66	Rd2	3	4	4	5	4	4	4	3	3	5	4	4	4	4	4	4	5	4	72		
	83	Rd3	4	4	5	5	5	5	6	3	4	3	3	4	5	5	5	4	5	4	79		
	T81	Rd4	4	4	4	4	5	4	4	2	3	4	3	3	4	5	4	4	4	4	69	+4	**292**
Sungjae Im	T35	Rd1	4	4	4	4	4	4	4	3	4	4	3	4	5	5	4	4	4	3	71		
Korea	T66	Rd2	4	3	4	4	6	4	4	3	3	3	3	4	4	6	5	4	5	4	73		
$31,200	T77	Rd3	4	5	4	4	5	4	5	3	3	4	3	4	5	5	4	5	4	3	74		
	T81	Rd4	4	5	4	4	5	4	4	3	4	4	3	5	4	4	4	5	4	4	74	+4	**292**
Jamie Rutherford	T77	Rd1	4	4	4	5	5	5	3	4	3	4	2	4	5	4	4	5	4	4	73		
England	T55	Rd2	3	4	3	4	5	4	3	3	4	4	3	3	5	5	4	4	6	3	70		
$31,075	82	Rd3	4	4	4	4	4	4	4	6	4	4	3	5	4	7	5	4	5	3	78		
	83	Rd4	5	4	4	5	4	4	4	3	4	4	3	4	5	5	4	4	6	3	75	+8	**296**

NON QUALIFIERS AFTER 36 HOLES

(Leading 10 professionals and ties receive $8,000 each, next 20 professionals and ties receive $6,500 each, remainder of professionals and ties receive $5,350 each)

HOLE			1	2	3	4	5	6	7	8	9	10	11	12	13	14	15	16	17	18			
PAR	POS		4	4	4	4	5	4	4	3	4	4	3	4	4	5	4	4	4	4	TOTAL		
Henrik Stenson	T119	Rd1	4	4	5	5	5	4	3	4	3	4	4	3	6	4	4	5	4	4	75		
Sweden	**T84**	Rd2	4	4	4	4	4	3	4	2	3	4	3	4	4	5	4	5	5	4	70	+1	**145**
Justin Harding	T101	Rd1	4	6	4	5	5	3	4	4	4	3	3	3	4	6	4	4	5	3	74		
South Africa	**T84**	Rd2	4	3	3	5	6	4	4	3	4	3	3	4	4	5	3	5	4	4	71	+1	**145**
Louis Oosthuizen	T35	Rd1	4	4	4	4	5	5	4	3	4	4	4	4	4	3	4	4	4	4	71		
South Africa	**T84**	Rd2	3	6	3	4	5	4	3	2	5	4	3	4	5	5	4	7	4	3	74	+1	**145**
Keith Mitchell	T133	Rd1	4	4	3	5	4	5	3	4	4	3	4	6	5	4	5	5	4	4	76		
USA	**T84**	Rd2	4	3	5	4	4	4	3	2	5	3	4	4	4	4	5	4	4	3	69	+1	**145**
Max Homa	T77	Rd1	4	5	4	4	5	4	4	3	4	4	3	3	4	5	5	4	5	3	73		
USA	**T84**	Rd2	4	4	6	4	4	5	4	2	3	4	4	4	4	5	4	4	4	3	72	+1	**145**
Webb Simpson	T35	Rd1	4	4	3	4	4	4	3	4	3	5	3	5	4	6	4	4	4	3	71		
USA	**T84**	Rd2	4	4	4	5	4	5	4	3	4	4	3	5	4	6	4	4	4	3	74	+1	**145**
Ben Campbell	T101	Rd1	4	4	5	4	5	3	5	3	4	4	3	5	4	4	3	5	6	3	74		
New Zealand	**T84**	Rd2	4	4	4	4	4	3	4	3	4	4	3	3	4	5	5	4	5	4	71	+1	**145**
Brandon Wu	T35	Rd1	4	4	4	4	4	4	3	3	3	3	4	4	5	6	4	4	4	4	71		
USA	**T84**	Rd2	4	3	4	4	4	4	5	4	3	4	3	4	4	6	4	4	6	4	74	+1	**145**
Jamie Donaldson	T133	Rd1	4	5	6	4	6	4	5	4	3	4	3	4	4	4	5	4	4	3	76		
Wales	**T84**	Rd2	4	4	4	5	5	3	3	3	3	4	3	3	4	6	4	4	4	3	69	+1	**145**
Ernie Els	T27	Rd1	3	3	4	5	5	4	4	2	3	4	2	3	4	5	4	5	6	4	70		
South Africa	**T84**	Rd2	4	5	4	5	5	4	4	3	4	4	3	5	4	5	4	4	4	4	75	+1	**145**
Scott Vincent	T13	Rd1	3	5	4	3	4	4	4	4	4	4	3	3	5	4	4	4	4	3	69		
Zimbabwe	**T84**	Rd2	5	4	5	4	5	4	4	3	4	3	3	4	6	4	4	6	4	4	76	+1	**145**
Collin Morikawa	T55	Rd1	4	5	4	4	4	4	5	3	3	3	3	4	5	5	4	5	4	3	72		
USA	**T84**	Rd2	4	5	4	4	4	4	4	4	5	4	3	5	4	4	4	4	4	3	73	+1	**145**
Takumi Kanaya	T101	Rd1	4	7	5	5	5	4	3	3	4	4	3	3	4	5	4	4	3	4	74		
Japan	**T84**	Rd2	4	4	4	4	5	4	3	3	3	4	3	4	5	5	4	4	4	4	71	+1	**145**
Zander Lombard	T143	Rd1	5	5	6	4	5	4	5	3	4	4	3	4	4	5	4	4	5	3	77		
South Africa	**T84**	Rd2	4	4	3	5	5	4	3	3	3	3	4	3	4	5	4	4	4	3	68	+1	**145**
Ryan Fox	T35	Rd1	4	4	4	5	4	4	4	3	4	5	3	3	4	4	4	4	4	4	71		
New Zealand	**T98**	Rd2	4	4	4	4	5	4	4	2	5	4	4	4	4	5	4	6	4	4	75	+2	**146**

HOLE			1	2	3	4	5	6	7	8	9	10	11	12	13	14	15	16	17	18			
PAR	POS		4	4	4	4	5	4	4	3	4	4	3	4	4	5	4	4	4	4			TOTAL
Richard Bland	T146	Rd1	4	4	4	4	7	5	5	3	5	4	3	6	4	4	4	5	4	3	78		
England	**T98**	Rd2	4	5	4	4	4	4	4	2	3	3	3	4	4	4	4	5	4	3	68	+2	**146**
Emiliano Grillo	T146	Rd1	5	4	4	5	5	4	5	3	4	4	4	4	4	5	4	5	6	3	78		
Argentina	**T98**	Rd2	3	5	5	3	4	4	4	4	3	3	3	4	4	4	4	5	3	3	68	+2	**146**
Matthew Griffin	T101	Rd1	4	5	4	5	5	4	4	3	4	4	3	3	5	5	4	4	5	3	74		
Australia	**T98**	Rd2	4	4	4	5	5	5	3	3	4	3	3	4	4	5	4	4	4	4	72	+2	**146**
Chan Kim	T101	Rd1	5	4	6	4	7	4	3	3	3	4	3	3	5	4	4	4	5	3	74		
USA	**T98**	Rd2	4	4	3	4	5	4	5	3	3	4	5	3	5	5	3	4	4	4	72	+2	**146**
Kyoung-Hoon Lee	T13	Rd1	4	4	4	5	5	3	4	3	3	4	3	4	4	4	4	3	4	4	69		
Korea	**T98**	Rd2	4	5	4	7	5	5	3	4	4	4	4	3	4	4	4	4	5	4	77	+2	**146**
JT Poston	T77	Rd1	3	3	3	5	5	4	4	3	3	4	4	5	5	6	3	4	6	3	73		
USA	**T98**	Rd2	5	4	3	5	4	5	4	3	5	3	3	3	5	4	5	5	4	3	73	+2	**146**
Matthew Jordan	T101	Rd1	4	4	4	5	5	4	4	3	3	4	4	6	4	4	4	5	5	3	74		
England	**T98**	Rd2	5	4	4	4	4	4	4	3	4	4	3	4	4	4	4	5	4	4	72	+2	**146**
Alexander Björk	T119	Rd1	3	5	4	5	5	4	4	3	4	4	3	5	5	5	4	5	4	3	75		
Sweden	**T98**	Rd2	4	3	5	3	3	4	4	4	4	5	3	4	5	4	4	4	4	4	71	+2	**146**
Shaun Norris	T101	Rd1	4	4	4	4	5	4	4	4	5	4	4	4	5	4	4	4	5	3	74		
South Africa	**T107**	Rd2	4	4	4	4	5	4	4	3	4	4	4	4	5	5	4	4	3	4	73	+3	**147**
Aaron Rai	T119	Rd1	4	4	5	6	5	4	4	3	4	4	4	3	4	4	5	4	4	4	75		
England	**T107**	Rd2	4	5	4	4	5	4	4	3	4	4	3	4	4	4	4	4	4	4	72	+3	**147**
Keita Nakajima[A]	T55	Rd1	5	5	5	3	5	4	4	3	4	3	3	3	5	4	4	5	4	3	72		
Japan	**T107**	Rd2	4	4	4	5	4	4	4	3	3	4	3	6	5	5	5	4	4	4	75	+3	**147**
Padraig Harrington	T13	Rd1	4	3	4	5	4	4	4	3	4	4	3	4	4	4	5	4	3		69		
Republic of Ireland	**T107**	Rd2	3	3	4	5	6	6	4	4	4	4	3	5	5	5	5	4	4	4	78	+3	**147**
Keegan Bradley	T133	Rd1	6	3	3	5	5	4	4	3	4	5	3	4	4	6	4	4	5	4	76		
USA	**T107**	Rd2	4	4	4	4	5	4	4	3	4	5	3	4	4	4	4	4	4	3	71	+3	**147**
John Catlin	T101	Rd1	5	4	5	5	7	3	4	3	3	5	4	3	4	5	4	3	4	3	74		
USA	**T107**	Rd2	4	4	4	4	5	4	4	3	4	4	4	3	5	5	4	5	4	3	73	+3	**147**
Guido Migliozzi	T77	Rd1	4	4	4	4	5	4	4	3	4	5	3	4	5	4	4	4	5	4	73		
Italy	**T107**	Rd2	4	5	4	4	5	4	4	3	3	3	4	3	5	6	4	5	4	4	74	+3	**147**
John Daly	T77	Rd1	4	5	4	5	4	5	4	2	4	4	4	3	4	5	3	5	5	3	73		
USA	**T107**	Rd2	3	4	4	5	3	4	3	4	5	3	4	4	5	4	4	5	5	5	74	+3	**147**
Zach Johnson	T55	Rd1	4	4	3	5	6	5	4	3	3	4	4	4	5	4	4	3	3	3	72		
USA	**T107**	Rd2	3	5	3	5	4	4	4	4	4	4	5	3	5	5	4	5	4	4	75	+3	**147**
Matt Ford	T35	Rd1	4	4	4	6	4	5	3	3	3	4	3	4	4	4	4	3	5	4	71		
England	**T107**	Rd2	4	5	5	3	6	5	4	3	3	4	4	4	3	6	5	4	4	4	76	+3	**147**
Bernd Wiesberger	T55	Rd1	4	4	5	4	4	3	4	3	3	5	4	4	5	5	4	4	4	3	72		
Austria	**T117**	Rd2	4	4	4	4	5	4	4	4	4	4	3	5	4	5	4	6	5	3	76	+4	**148**
Kevin Na	T55	Rd1	4	4	4	4	5	4	4	3	4	4	3	4	5	4	5	4	5	3	72		
USA	**T117**	Rd2	5	5	4	5	5	4	4	4	3	4	5	5	4	4	5	4	4	2	76	+4	**148**
Mingyu Cho	T119	Rd1	3	4	4	5	5	4	4	3	4	4	3	4	5	5	4	7	4	3	75		
Korea	**T117**	Rd2	4	4	4	4	5	4	4	3	3	4	3	4	5	5	5	5	4	3	73	+4	**148**
Ashley Chesters	T119	Rd1	4	4	4	5	5	4	4	3	5	3	4	4	4	5	4	5	5	4	75		
England	**T117**	Rd2	4	4	3	5	5	4	3	3	5	3	4	4	5	4	5	4	4	4	73	+4	**148**
Brooks Koepka	T77	Rd1	4	5	4	4	5	4	3	3	5	3	3	4	5	4	5	4	3	4	73		
USA	**T117**	Rd2	5	5	3	4	4	4	4	3	5	3	3	3	4	6	4	4	6	5	75	+4	**148**
Seamus Power	T77	Rd1	3	5	4	5	5	4	4	3	3	3	3	6	4	5	4	4	5	3	73		
Republic of Ireland	**T117**	Rd2	5	5	4	4	5	4	4	3	4	4	4	3	4	5	5	4	4	4	75	+4	**148**

	POS		1	2	3	4	5	6	7	8	9	10	11	12	13	14	15	16	17	18		TOTAL
Rikuya Hoshino	T119	Rd1	4	4	4	4	6	4	4	4	3	4	3	3	5	5	4	5	6	3	75	
Japan	**T117**	Rd2	4	4	4	5	4	6	4	3	4	4	3	4	4	4	4	4	4	4	73	+4 **148**
Mackenzie Hughes	T77	Rd1	4	4	4	4	6	4	4	2	4	3	3	3	6	6	4	4	4	4	73	
Canada	**T117**	Rd2	4	5	3	3	4	4	5	3	4	3	4	3	4	6	5	5	6	4	75	+4 **148**
Haotong Li	T77	Rd1	4	5	4	4	4	4	4	2	7	3	4	3	4	6	4	4	4	3	73	
China	**T125**	Rd2	7	4	4	4	4	4	4	3	4	3	5	4	4	5	4	4	5	4	76	+5 **149**
Fabrizio Zanotti	T55	Rd1	5	5	4	5	4	4	4	3	3	4	3	3	5	4	4	4	4	4	72	
Paraguay	**T125**	Rd2	4	4	5	4	5	4	4	4	4	4	3	4	4	6	5	4	5	4	77	+5 **149**
Stewart Cink	T146	Rd1	5	4	4	4	5	5	4	4	5	4	3	4	4	4	4	5	5	5	78	
USA	**T125**	Rd2	4	3	4	4	5	4	4	3	3	4	3	5	4	5	3	5	5	3	71	+5 **149**
Kazuki Higa	T77	Rd1	4	5	3	5	5	3	4	4	4	4	3	3	4	5	5	4	4	4	73	
Japan	**T125**	Rd2	3	5	4	4	5	4	4	3	5	4	3	5	5	6	4	5	4	3	76	+5 **149**
Mito Pereira	T119	Rd1	4	5	3	5	5	4	3	3	3	3	4	7	6	4	4	4	4	4	75	
Chile	**T125**	Rd2	3	5	4	4	4	5	4	3	3	4	5	5	4	5	4	5	4	3	74	+5 **149**
Phil Mickelson	T55	Rd1	4	4	4	4	5	4	3	3	4	5	4	3	5	4	4	4	4	4	72	
USA	**T125**	Rd2	4	4	3	4	5	5	4	4	4	4	3	5	6	5	4	5	5	3	77	+5 **149**
Luke List	T133	Rd1	4	5	4	4	6	4	4	3	4	4	3	4	5	6	4	4	4	4	76	
USA	**T125**	Rd2	4	5	4	5	4	4	4	3	4	4	4	4	4	5	3	3	5	4	73	+5 **149**
Sihwan Kim	T133	Rd1	5	4	4	6	4	4	4	3	3	4	3	5	5	4	5	4	5	4	76	
USA	**T125**	Rd2	4	4	3	4	5	4	3	3	3	3	4	5	5	4	4	4	4	6	73	+5 **149**
Marco Penge	T133	Rd1	4	5	5	4	4	4	5	3	5	4	3	6	4	5	4	4	3	4	76	
England	**T125**	Rd2	4	6	3	5	5	4	4	3	4	4	3	3	4	4	4	4	5	4	73	+5 **149**
Aldrich Potgieter[A]	T101	Rd1	4	4	4	4	6	4	4	3	4	4	3	5	6	4	4	4	4	3	74	
South Africa	**T134**	Rd2	4	3	4	4	4	5	5	3	5	4	4	4	5	5	4	5	5	3	76	+6 **150**
Gary Woodland	T101	Rd1	4	4	4	5	5	3	4	4	4	5	4	4	5	4	4	4	4	3	74	
USA	**T134**	Rd2	4	5	4	4	5	4	4	4	4	5	5	4	3	4	5	4	4	4	76	+6 **150**
Marc Leishman	T133	Rd1	3	4	3	5	5	5	4	3	3	4	4	6	5	5	4	5	5	3	76	
Australia	**T134**	Rd2	6	5	5	4	5	4	4	2	3	4	6	3	4	4	4	4	3	4	74	+6 **150**
Harris English	T133	Rd1	5	5	6	4	3	4	4	4	5	3	3	3	5	4	5	6	3	4	76	
USA	**T134**	Rd2	4	5	4	5	5	4	4	3	2	4	3	3	4	6	4	4	4	6	74	+6 **150**
Minkyu Kim	T77	Rd1	3	4	4	5	4	5	4	3	3	4	3	5	5	4	5	4	4	3	73	
Korea	**T134**	Rd2	5	4	4	4	4	4	4	3	3	4	6	4	5	5	5	4	5	4	77	+6 **150**
Tom Hoge	T101	Rd1	4	4	4	3	5	4	4	3	3	3	6	3	6	4	4	5	5	4	74	
USA	**T134**	Rd2	5	5	3	4	4	3	4	4	5	3	3	4	5	5	4	4	6	5	76	+6 **150**
Oliver Farr	T133	Rd1	4	4	4	4	5	4	4	3	4	4	3	4	6	5	5	5	4	4	76	
Wales	**T134**	Rd2	4	4	4	4	6	5	3	3	5	3	3	5	4	5	4	3	5	4	74	+6 **150**
Dimitrios Papadatos	T143	Rd1	4	4	4	6	5	5	5	3	4	4	3	4	4	5	4	5	5	3	77	
Australia	**T141**	Rd2	4	4	4	5	4	4	4	3	4	4	5	3	4	5	5	4	4	4	74	+7 **151**
Jorge Fernández Valdés	T101	Rd1	4	4	6	4	5	4	4	4	4	4	4	4	4	4	4	4	4	3	74	
Argentina	**T141**	Rd2	4	4	3	5	5	4	4	3	4	4	4	5	5	5	5	5	5	4	77	+7 **151**
Ronan Mullarney	T77	Rd1	4	4	5	4	3	4	3	2	4	4	4	5	5	4	5	4	5	4	73	
Republic of Ireland	**T141**	Rd2	4	4	4	5	6	4	4	4	5	3	5	3	4	5	5	5	4	4	78	+7 **151**
Paul Lawrie	T101	Rd1	4	5	4	6	4	4	4	3	3	4	3	5	5	4	4	5	5	2	74	
Scotland	**T141**	Rd2	4	4	4	5	5	4	5	3	5	3	3	4	4	6	5	4	5	4	77	+7 **151**
Stephen Dodd	T143	Rd1	5	4	4	5	4	5	3	3	3	4	4	5	5	5	6	5	3	77		
Wales	**T141**	Rd2	5	4	4	5	4	5	4	3	4	3	3	4	5	5	5	3	4	4	74	+7 **151**

HOLE			1	2	3	4	5	6	7	8	9	10	11	12	13	14	15	16	17	18	
PAR	POS		4	4	4	4	5	4	4	3	4	4	3	4	4	5	4	4	4	4	TOTAL
Sam Horsfield	T133	Rd1	5	5	4	5	4	4	4	4	4	4	4	3	5	5	5	4	4	3	76
England	**T146**	Rd2	6	4	4	4	4	3	4	4	5	5	3	5	5	4	4	5	4	3	76 +8 **152**
Shugo Imahira	152	Rd1	5	6	5	5	6	4	5	3	4	4	3	5	4	6	3	4	5	3	80
Japan	**T146**	Rd2	4	4	4	4	5	4	4	3	4	3	4	4	5	4	4	6	3		72 +8 **152**
Tiger Woods	T146	Rd1	6	4	5	5	5	4	6	3	3	3	4	4	5	4	4	5	4	4	78
USA	**T148**	Rd2	4	4	3	5	5	5	4	3	4	4	3	4	4	5	4	6	4	4	75 +9 **153**
Sepp Straka	153	Rd1	4	4	5	5	5	4	4	3	5	5	3	5	5	5	5	6	4	4	81
Austria	**T148**	Rd2	4	4	4	4	5	4	4	4	4	4	4	3	4	4	4	5	4	3	72 +9 **153**
Darren Clarke	T150	Rd1	4	6	4	5	6	5	4	3	4	4	3	4	5	4	4	6	4		79
Northern Ireland	**T150**	Rd2	4	5	4	5	4	3	4	3	4	4	3	4	4	6	5	5	4	4	75 +10 **154**
Jack Floydd	T119	Rd1	4	4	4	5	5	4	4	3	3	4	4	3	6	6	4	4	4	4	75
England	**T150**	Rd2	4	5	4	5	4	6	4	3	4	4	4	5	4	5	4	7	4	3	79 +10 **154**
Jediah Morgan	T150	Rd1	5	4	4	5	5	4	4	3	4	4	3	7	5	5	5	5	4	3	79
Australia	**T152**	Rd2	5	4	4	5	5	4	4	3	4	4	3	4	5	5	4	5	4	4	76 +11 **155**
Alex Wrigley	T154	Rd1	6	4	4	5	5	6	4	3	4	3	4	4	6	7	4	4	5	4	82
England	**T152**	Rd2	4	5	4	4	5	4	4	3	4	4	3	4	5	4	4	4	4	4	73 +11 **155**
David Duval	T154	Rd1	4	5	4	5	6	6	5	3	5	4	4	4	5	4	4	4	5	5	82
USA	**T154**	Rd2	4	5	4	4	4	4	4	3	4	4	3	5	4	5	4	4	4	5	74 +12 **156**
Pablo Larrazabal	T119	Rd1	4	4	4	5	5	5	4	3	4	4	4	4	5	4	3	6	4	3	75
Spain	**T154**	Rd2	4	4	5	5	5	6	5	3	5	4	3	4	4	5	3	5	7	4	81 +12 **156**
Mark Calcavecchia	156	Rd1	6	4	4	4	6	5	4	3	3	5	3	4	6	5	5	5	7	4	83
USA	**156**	Rd2	4	5	5	5	6	5	4	4	4	3	3	5	5	5	4	6	4	5	82 +21 **165**

THE TOP TENS

Driving Distance

1. **Adri Arnaus** 346.2
2. Nicolai Højgaard 345.5
3. Justin Thomas 344.0
4. Rory McIlroy 343.8
5. Thomas Detry 342.7
6. Will Zalatoris 340.9
7. Dustin Johnson 340.2
8. Xander Schauffele 339.4
9. Anthony Quayle 339.1
10. Min Woo Lee 338.6
61. *Cameron Smith* 317.0

Fairways Hit

Maximum of 64

1. **Abraham Ancer** 49
1. Corey Conners 49
3. Bryson DeChambeau 48
3. Billy Horschel 48
5. Chris Kirk 47
5. Yuto Katsuragawa 47
5. Joohyung Kim 47
8. Brian Harman 46
8. Francesco Molinari 46
8. Victor Perez 46
8. Brad Kennedy 46
24. *Cameron Smith* 43

Greens in Regulation

Maximum of 72

1. **Bryson DeChambeau** 66
2. Rory McIlroy 65
3. Yuto Katsuragawa 64
3. Adri Arnaus 64
5. *Cameron Smith* 63
6. Patrick Cantlay 62
6. Abraham Ancer 62
6. Scottie Scheffler 62
6. Russell Henley 62
10. Billy Horschel 61
10. Shane Lowry 61
10. Matt Fitzpatrick 61

Putts

1. **Si Woo Kim** 119
2. *Cameron Smith* 120
2. Brian Harman 120
2. Dylan Frittelli 120
5. Viktor Hovland 121
5. Duston Johnson 121
5. Patrick Reed 121
5. Marcus Armitage 121
9. Dean Burmester 122
9. Adam Scott 122
9. Brad Kennedy 122
9. Sergio Garcia 122
9. Barclay Brown[A] 122

STATISTICAL RANKINGS

	Driving Distance	Rank	Fairways Hit	Rank	Greens In Regulation	Rank	Putts	Rank
Abraham Ancer	335.4	16	49	1	62	6	126	32
Marcus Armitage	317.1	60	35	78	47	82	121	5
Adri Arnaus	346.2	1	39	56	64	3	138	81
Sam Bairstow[(A)]	329.3	29	39	56	46	83	126	32
Christiaan Bezuidenhout	314.6	66	37	71	55	63	127	41
Barclay Brown[(A)]	313.9	68	33	83	50	81	122	9
Dean Burmester	323.3	43	36	74	56	56	122	9
Sam Burns	325.9	37	35	78	57	44	123	14
Laurie Canter	314.7	64	39	56	51	77	126	32
Patrick Cantlay	315.7	63	40	46	62	6	127	41
David Carey	337.5	11	36	74	54	70	131	65
Paul Casey	327.1	34	41	34	60	13	128	47
Filippo Celli[(A)]	329.0	30	45	12	53	75	130	60
Wyndham Clark	331.0	22	38	67	51	77	133	74
Corey Conners	314.6	66	49	1	58	31	124	21
Justin De Los Santos	319.0	54	39	56	58	31	131	65
Bryson DeChambeau	327.8	31	48	3	66	1	132	72
Thomas Detry	342.7	5	41	34	56	56	126	32
Robert Dinwiddie	317.9	57	40	46	57	44	128	47
Tony Finau	325.7	38	38	67	57	44	124	21
Matt Fitzpatrick	330.9	24	39	56	61	10	128	47
Tommy Fleetwood	331.7	21	39	56	60	13	124	21
Dylan Frittelli	313.3	70	38	67	55	63	120	2
Sergio Garcia	321.8	48	39	56	51	77	122	9
Talor Gooch	330.7	25	45	12	59	24	131	65
Brian Harman	302.9	82	46	8	57	44	120	2
Tyrrell Hatton	336.7	12	44	19	58	31	124	21
Russell Henley	312.7	71	45	12	62	6	133	74
Lucas Herbert	330.4	27	42	28	56	56	123	14
Garrick Higgo	318.5	55	42	28	57	44	125	30
Nicolai Højgaard	345.5	2	39	56	58	31	128	47
Billy Horschel	311.6	72	48	3	61	10	130	60
Viktor Hovland	327.5	32	39	56	58	31	121	5
Sungjae Im	327.1	34	45	12	59	24	142	83
Aaron Jarvis[(A)]	307.6	77	41	34	55	63	132	72
Dustin Johnson	340.2	7	41	34	60	13	121	5
Sadom Kaewkanjana	305.1	79	44	19	59	24	123	14
Yuto Katsuragawa	319.8	51	47	5	64	3	135	78
Brad Kennedy	311.1	73	46	8	54	70	122	9
Si Woo Kim	318.1	56	41	34	54	70	119	1
Joohyung Kim	314.7	64	47	5	58	31	130	60
Chris Kirk	322.6	45	47	5	56	56	124	21
Kevin Kisner	305.4	78	42	28	60	13	126	32
Kurt Kitayama	323.0	44	34	81	56	54	129	55
Jason Kokrak	323.9	42	41	34	56	56	125	30
David Law	322.5	46	38	67	53	75	131	65
Thriston Lawrence	334.0	18	39	56	58	31	128	47
Min Woo Lee	338.6	10	40	46	59	24	127	41
Shane Lowry	330.4	27	43	24	61	10	128	47
Robert MacIntyre	321.2	50	35	78	55	63	123	14
Richard Mansell	327.2	33	39	56	59	24	136	80
Hideki Matsuyama	313.7	69	45	12	57	44	131	65
Rory McIlroy	343.8	4	41	34	65	2	129	55
Adrian Meronk	325.6	39	36	74	58	31	129	55
Francesco Molinari	309.7	74	46	8	59	24	123	14
Trey Mullinax	324.7	41	40	46	60	13	128	47
Sebastián Muñoz	319.1	53	45	12	57	44	127	41
Joaquin Niemann	335.8	15	36	74	56	56	129	55
John Parry	316.0	62	40	46	54	70	124	21
Victor Perez	330.7	25	46	8	60	13	131	65
Thomas Pieters	332.1	20	34	82	56	56	124	21
Ian Poulter	309.0	75	42	27	56	54	126	32
Anthony Quayle	339.1	9	45	12	57	44	126	32
Jon Rahm	336.4	13	41	34	60	13	131	65
Patrick Reed	303.8	80	37	71	54	70	121	5
Jamie Rutherford	299.8	83	42	28	59	24	140	82
Xander Schauffele	339.4	8	41	34	58	31	128	47
Scottie Scheffler	321.4	49	44	19	62	6	126	32
Adam Scott	325.5	40	44	19	55	63	122	9
Jason Scrivener	303.8	80	37	71	60	13	133	74
Cameron Smith	317.0	61	43	24	63	5	120	2
Jordan Smith	332.8	19	40	46	58	31	135	78
Jordan Spieth	317.4	59	41	34	60	13	124	21
Sahith Theegala	335.9	14	40	46	60	13	130	60
Justin Thomas	344.0	3	42	28	57	44	129	55
Cameron Tringale	308.3	76	44	19	58	31	130	60
Lars Van Meijel	331.0	22	41	34	51	77	124	21
Harold Varner III	326.6	36	40	46	57	44	126	32
Lee Westwood	317.6	58	42	28	55	63	123	14
Danny Willett	319.8	51	43	24	55	63	127	41
Aaron Wise	322.2	47	40	46	58	31	133	74
Cameron Young	334.6	17	41	34	60	13	123	14
Will Zalatoris	340.9	6	40	46	58	31	127	41

NON QUALIFIERS AFTER 36 HOLES

	Driving Distance	Rank	Fairways Hit	Rank	Greens In Regulation	Rank	Putts	Rank
Alexander Björk	322.1	64	17	134	28	70	67	96
Richard Bland	316.5	79	21	51	26	108	65	59
Keegan Bradley	326.0	47	18	111	27	97	67	96
Mark Calcavecchia	284.0	154	18	111	21	154	73	153
Ben Campbell	285.7	152	19	92	22	147	60	9
John Catlin	324.7	56	25	3	29	39	74	154
Ashley Chesters	297.8	139	22	29	28	70	68	112
Mingyu Cho	303.2	127	17	134	28	70	70	131
Stewart Cink	333.1	26	22	29	28	70	71	143
Darren Clarke	308.2	115	18	111	20	155	63	32
John Daly	308.5	114	22	29	24	134	65	59
Stephen Dodd	315.5	86	18	111	23	142	64	44
Jamie Donaldson	283.9	155	22	29	27	97	66	75
David Duval	307.8	116	16	148	18	156	67	96
Ernie Els	303.1	129	19	92	30	24	71	143
Harris English	339.5	14	22	29	22	147	66	75
Oliver Farr	314.6	88	21	51	26	108	70	131
Jorge Fernández Valdés	310.7	104	17	134	25	126	66	75
Jack Floydd	306.4	120	18	111	22	147	65	59
Matt Ford	296.4	143	17	134	28	70	67	96
Ryan Fox	326.7	41	19	92	31	13	71	143
Matthew Griffin	315.9	81	21	51	27	97	66	75
Emiliano Grillo	321.6	68	18	111	22	147	64	44
Justin Harding	319.7	75	21	51	29	39	66	75
Padraig Harrington	322.4	63	16	148	28	70	68	112
Kazuki Higa	325.8	49	18	111	26	108	67	96
Tom Hoge	309.3	107	22	29	29	39	70	131
Max Homa	347.8	4	17	134	28	70	67	96
Sam Horsfield	341.4	12	22	29	23	142	70	131
Rikuya Hoshino	303.0	130	19	92	26	108	68	112
Mackenzie Hughes	315.8	82	17	134	27	97	67	96
Shugo Imahira	296.3	144	16	148	22	147	67	96
Zach Johnson	295.1	146	27	1	26	108	66	75
Matthew Jordan	312.7	96	18	111	30	24	68	112
Takumi Kanaya	326.3	44	25	3	29	39	68	112
Chan Kim	323.9	60	22	29	29	39	69	126
Sihwan Kim	309.2	108	17	134	24	134	63	32
Minkyu Kim	294.0	147	22	29	28	70	70	131
Brooks Koepka	312.2	98	18	111	27	97	67	96
Pablo Larrazabal	302.9	131	19	92	28	70	74	154

	Driving Distance	Rank	Fairways Hit	Rank	Greens In Regulation	Rank	Putts	Rank
Paul Lawrie	298.0	138	22	29	26	108	71	143
Kyoung-Hoon Lee	314.6	88	21	51	26	108	62	19
Marc Leishman	344.7	8	20	77	26	108	67	96
Haotong Li	288.8	151	16	148	25	126	63	32
Luke List	325.4	51	16	148	26	108	66	75
Zander Lombard	324.9	54	22	29	28	70	66	75
Phil Mickelson	295.2	145	19	92	26	108	67	96
Guido Migliozzi	291.5	150	24	7	28	70	69	126
Keith Mitchell	333.8	24	19	92	27	97	66	75
Jediah Morgan	307.6	118	18	111	25	126	71	143
Collin Morikawa	335.6	19	20	77	25	126	65	59
Ronan Mullarney	284.7	153	20	77	22	147	68	112
Kevin Na	321.9	66	22	29	22	147	64	44
Keita Nakajima[A]	315.6	85	18	111	23	142	65	59
Shaun Norris	324.9	54	25	3	29	39	69	126
Louis Oosthuizen	328.6	34	19	92	28	70	68	112
Dimitrios Papadatos	309.2	108	17	134	27	97	70	131
Marco Penge	347.7	5	17	134	29	39	71	143
Mito Pereira	315.7	83	18	111	29	39	69	126
JT Poston	321.9	66	18	111	26	108	64	44
Aldrich Potgieter[A]	332.3	28	15	155	26	108	68	112
Seamus Power	316.7	78	19	92	25	126	66	75
Aaron Rai	297.4	141	21	51	24	134	63	32
Webb Simpson	311.2	103	27	1	28	70	65	59
Henrik Stenson	297.1	142	23	20	28	70	66	75
Sepp Straka	324.7	56	22	29	24	134	66	75
Scott Vincent	334.6	23	19	92	32	5	71	143
Bernd Wiesberger	327.5	38	17	134	29	39	70	131
Gary Woodland	309.0	111	20	77	29	39	72	150
Tiger Woods	338.9	15	21	51	26	108	70	131
Alex Wrigley	312.2	98	21	51	26	108	72	150
Brandon Wu	312.2	98	24	7	29	39	68	112
Fabrizio Zanotti	314.0	93	23	20	31	13	75	156

ROLL OF HONOUR

Year	Champion	Score	Margin	Runners-up	Venue
1860	Willie Park Sr	174	2	Tom Morris Sr	Prestwick
1861	Tom Morris Sr	163	4	Willie Park Sr	Prestwick
1862	Tom Morris Sr	163	13	Willie Park Sr	Prestwick
1863	Willie Park Sr	168	2	Tom Morris Sr	Prestwick
1864	Tom Morris Sr	167	2	Andrew Strath	Prestwick
1865	Andrew Strath	162	2	Willie Park Sr	Prestwick
1866	Willie Park Sr	169	2	David Park	Prestwick
1867	Tom Morris Sr	170	2	Willie Park Sr	Prestwick
1868	Tommy Morris Jr	154	3	Tom Morris Sr	Prestwick
1869	Tommy Morris Jr	157	11	Bob Kirk	Prestwick
1870	Tommy Morris Jr	149	12	Bob Kirk, Davie Strath	Prestwick
1871	*No Championship*				
1872	Tommy Morris Jr	166	3	Davie Strath	Prestwick
1873	Tom Kidd	179	1	Jamie Anderson	St Andrews
1874	Mungo Park	159	2	Tommy Morris Jr	Musselburgh
1875	Willie Park Sr	166	2	Bob Martin	Prestwick
1876	Bob Martin	176	–	Davie Strath	St Andrews
	(Martin was awarded the title when Strath refused to play-off)				
1877	Jamie Anderson	160	2	Bob Pringle	Musselburgh
1878	Jamie Anderson	157	2	Bob Kirk	Prestwick
1879	Jamie Anderson	169	3	Jamie Allan, Andrew Kirkaldy	St Andrews
1880	Bob Ferguson	162	5	Peter Paxton	Musselburgh
1881	Bob Ferguson	170	3	Jamie Anderson	Prestwick
1882	Bob Ferguson	171	3	Willie Fernie	St Andrews
1883	Willie Fernie	158	Play-off	Bob Ferguson	Musselburgh
1884	Jack Simpson	160	4	Douglas Rolland, Willie Fernie	Prestwick
1885	Bob Martin	171	1	Archie Simpson	St Andrews
1886	David Brown	157	2	Willie Campbell	Musselburgh
1887	Willie Park Jr	161	1	Bob Martin	Prestwick
1888	Jack Burns	171	1	David Anderson Jr, Ben Sayers	St Andrews
1889	Willie Park Jr	155	Play-off	Andrew Kirkaldy	Musselburgh
1890	John Ball Jr[A]	164	3	Willie Fernie, Archie Simpson	Prestwick
1891	Hugh Kirkaldy	166	2	Willie Fernie, Andrew Kirkaldy	St Andrews
	(From 1892 the Championship was extended to 72 holes)				
1892	Harold Hilton[A]	305	3	John Ball Jr[A], Hugh Kirkaldy, Sandy Herd	Muirfield
1893	Willie Auchterlonie	322	2	John Laidlay[A]	Prestwick

Champion Golfers dating from Gary Player (1959) to Collin Morikawa (2021) gathered for dinner on Tuesday night.

Year	Champion	Score	Margin	Runners-up	Venue
1894	JH Taylor	326	5	Douglas Rolland	St George's
1895	JH Taylor	322	4	Sandy Herd	St Andrews
1896	Harry Vardon	316	Play-off	JH Taylor	Muirfield
1897	Harold Hilton[A]	314	1	James Braid	Royal Liverpool
1898	Harry Vardon	307	1	Willie Park Jr	Prestwick
1899	Harry Vardon	310	5	Jack White	St George's
1900	JH Taylor	309	8	Harry Vardon	St Andrews
1901	James Braid	309	3	Harry Vardon	Muirfield
1902	Sandy Herd	307	1	Harry Vardon, James Braid	Royal Liverpool
1903	Harry Vardon	300	6	Tom Vardon	Prestwick
1904	Jack White	296	1	James Braid, JH Taylor	Royal St George's
1905	James Braid	318	5	JH Taylor, Rowland Jones	St Andrews
1906	James Braid	300	4	JH Taylor	Muirfield
1907	Arnaud Massy	312	2	JH Taylor	Royal Liverpool
1908	James Braid	291	8	Tom Ball	Prestwick
1909	JH Taylor	295	6	James Braid, Tom Ball	Cinque Ports
1910	James Braid	299	4	Sandy Herd	St Andrews
1911	Harry Vardon	303	Play-off	Arnaud Massy	Royal St George's
1912	Ted Ray	295	4	Harry Vardon	Muirfield
1913	JH Taylor	304	8	Ted Ray	Royal Liverpool
1914	Harry Vardon	306	3	JH Taylor	Prestwick
1915-1919 *No Championship*					
1920	George Duncan	303	2	Sandy Herd	Royal Cinque Ports
1921	Jock Hutchison	296	Play-off	Roger Wethered[A]	St Andrews
1922	Walter Hagen	300	1	George Duncan, Jim Barnes	Royal St George's

Year	Champion	Score	Margin	Runners-up	Venue
1923	Arthur Havers	295	1	Walter Hagen	Troon
1924	Walter Hagen	301	1	Ernest Whitcombe	Royal Liverpool
1925	Jim Barnes	300	1	Archie Compston, Ted Ray	Prestwick
1926	Bobby Jones[(A)]	291	2	Al Watrous	Royal Lytham
1927	Bobby Jones[(A)]	285	6	Aubrey Boomer, Fred Robson	St Andrews
1928	Walter Hagen	292	2	Gene Sarazen	Royal St George's
1929	Walter Hagen	292	6	Johnny Farrell	Muirfield
1930	Bobby Jones[(A)]	291	2	Leo Diegel, Macdonald Smith	Royal Liverpool
1931	Tommy Armour	296	1	Jose Jurado	Carnoustie
1932	Gene Sarazen	283	5	Macdonald Smith	Prince's
1933	Denny Shute	292	Play-off	Craig Wood	St Andrews
1934	Henry Cotton	283	5	Sid Brews	Royal St George's
1935	Alf Perry	283	4	Alf Padgham	Muirfield
1936	Alf Padgham	287	1	Jimmy Adams	Royal Liverpool
1937	Henry Cotton	290	2	Reg Whitcombe	Carnoustie
1938	Reg Whitcombe	295	2	Jimmy Adams	Royal St George's
1939	Dick Burton	290	2	Johnny Bulla	St Andrews

1940-1945 No Championship

Year	Champion	Score	Margin	Runners-up	Venue
1946	Sam Snead	290	4	Bobby Locke, Johnny Bulla	St Andrews
1947	Fred Daly	293	1	Reg Horne, Frank Stranahan[(A)]	Royal Liverpool
1948	Henry Cotton	284	5	Fred Daly	Muirfield
1949	Bobby Locke	283	Play-off	Harry Bradshaw	Royal St George's
1950	Bobby Locke	279	2	Roberto de Vicenzo	Troon
1951	Max Faulkner	285	2	Antonio Cerda	Royal Portrush
1952	Bobby Locke	287	1	Peter Thomson	Royal Lytham
1953	Ben Hogan	282	4	Frank Stranahan[(A)], Dai Rees, Peter Thomson, Antonio Cerda	Carnoustie
1954	Peter Thomson	283	1	Syd Scott, Dai Rees, Bobby Locke	Royal Birkdale
1955	Peter Thomson	281	2	John Fallon	St Andrews
1956	Peter Thomson	286	3	Flory Van Donck	Royal Liverpool
1957	Bobby Locke	279	3	Peter Thomson	St Andrews
1958	Peter Thomson	278	Play-off	Dave Thomas	Royal Lytham
1959	Gary Player	284	2	Flory Van Donck, Fred Bullock	Muirfield
1960	Kel Nagle	278	1	Arnold Palmer	St Andrews
1961	Arnold Palmer	284	1	Dai Rees	Royal Birkdale
1962	Arnold Palmer	276	6	Kel Nagle	Troon

(Prior to 1963, scores assessed against "level 4s". From 1963, pars were introduced and holes were played in 3, 4 or 5 shots.)

Year	Champion	To Par	Score	Margin	Runners-up	Venue
1963	Bob Charles	-3	277	Play-off	Phil Rodgers	Royal Lytham
1964	Tony Lema	-9	279	5	Jack Nicklaus	St Andrews
1965	Peter Thomson	-7	285	2	Christy O'Connor Sr, Brian Huggett	Royal Birkdale
1966	Jack Nicklaus	-2	282	1	Dave Thomas, Doug Sanders	Muirfield
1967	Roberto de Vicenzo	-10	278	2	Jack Nicklaus	Royal Liverpool
1968	Gary Player	+1	289	2	Jack Nicklaus, Bob Charles	Carnoustie
1969	Tony Jacklin	-4	280	2	Bob Charles	Royal Lytham
1970	Jack Nicklaus	-5	283	Play-off	Doug Sanders	St Andrews
1971	Lee Trevino	-14	278	1	Liang Huan Lu	Royal Birkdale
1972	Lee Trevino	-6	278	1	Jack Nicklaus	Muirfield
1973	Tom Weiskopf	-12	276	3	Neil Coles, Johnny Miller	Troon
1974	Gary Player	-2	282	4	Peter Oosterhuis	Royal Lytham
1975	Tom Watson	-9	279	Play-off	Jack Newton	Carnoustie
1976	Johnny Miller	-9	279	6	Jack Nicklaus, Seve Ballesteros	Royal Birkdale
1977	Tom Watson	-12	268	1	Jack Nicklaus	Turnberry

Year	Champion	To Par	Score	Margin	Runners-up	Venue
1978	Jack Nicklaus	-7	281	2	Simon Owen, Ben Crenshaw, Ray Floyd, Tom Kite	St Andrews
1979	Seve Ballesteros	-1	283	3	Jack Nicklaus, Ben Crenshaw	Royal Lytham
1980	Tom Watson	-13	271	4	Lee Trevino	Muirfield
1981	Bill Rogers	-4	276	4	Bernhard Langer	Royal St George's
1982	Tom Watson	-4	284	1	Peter Oosterhuis, Nick Price	Royal Troon
1983	Tom Watson	-9	275	1	Hale Irwin, Andy Bean	Royal Birkdale
1984	Seve Ballesteros	-12	276	2	Bernhard Langer, Tom Watson	St Andrews
1985	Sandy Lyle	+2	282	1	Payne Stewart	Royal St George's
1986	Greg Norman	E	280	5	Gordon J Brand	Turnberry
1987	Nick Faldo	-5	279	1	Rodger Davis, Paul Azinger	Muirfield
1988	Seve Ballesteros	-11	273	2	Nick Price	Royal Lytham
1989	Mark Calcavecchia	-13	275	Play-off	Greg Norman, Wayne Grady	Royal Troon
1990	Nick Faldo	-18	270	5	Mark McNulty, Payne Stewart	St Andrews
1991	Ian Baker-Finch	-8	272	2	Mike Harwood	Royal Birkdale
1992	Nick Faldo	-12	272	1	John Cook	Muirfield
1993	Greg Norman	-13	267	2	Nick Faldo	Royal St George's
1994	Nick Price	-12	268	1	Jesper Parnevik	Turnberry
1995	John Daly	-6	282	Play-off	Costantino Rocca	St Andrews
1996	Tom Lehman	-13	271	2	Mark McCumber, Ernie Els	Royal Lytham
1997	Justin Leonard	-12	272	3	Jesper Parnevik, Darren Clarke	Royal Troon
1998	Mark O'Meara	E	280	Play-off	Brian Watts	Royal Birkdale
1999	Paul Lawrie	+6	290	Play-off	Justin Leonard, Jean van de Velde	Carnoustie
2000	Tiger Woods	-19	269	8	Ernie Els, Thomas Bjørn	St Andrews
2001	David Duval	-10	274	3	Niclas Fasth	Royal Lytham
2002	Ernie Els	-6	278	Play-off	Thomas Levet, Stuart Appleby, Steve Elkington	Muirfield
2003	Ben Curtis	-1	283	1	Thomas Bjørn, Vijay Singh	Royal St George's
2004	Todd Hamilton	-10	274	Play-off	Ernie Els	Royal Troon
2005	Tiger Woods	-14	274	5	Colin Montgomerie	St Andrews
2006	Tiger Woods	-18	270	2	Chris DiMarco	Royal Liverpool
2007	Padraig Harrington	-7	277	Play-off	Sergio Garcia	Carnoustie
2008	Padraig Harrington	+3	283	4	Ian Poulter	Royal Birkdale
2009	Stewart Cink	-2	278	Play-off	Tom Watson	Turnberry
2010	Louis Oosthuizen	-16	272	7	Lee Westwood	St Andrews
2011	Darren Clarke	-5	275	3	Phil Mickelson, Dustin Johnson	Royal St George's
2012	Ernie Els	-7	273	1	Adam Scott	Royal Lytham
2013	Phil Mickelson	-3	281	3	Henrik Stenson	Muirfield
2014	Rory McIlroy	-17	271	2	Sergio Garcia, Rickie Fowler	Royal Liverpool
2015	Zach Johnson	-15	273	Play-off	Louis Oosthuizen, Marc Leishman	St Andrews
2016	Henrik Stenson	-20	264	3	Phil Mickelson	Royal Troon
2017	Jordan Spieth	-12	268	3	Matt Kuchar	Royal Birkdale
2018	Francesco Molinari	-8	276	2	Justin Rose, Rory McIlroy, Kevin Kisner, Xander Schauffele	Carnoustie
2019	Shane Lowry	-15	269	6	Tommy Fleetwood	Royal Portrush
2020	*No Championship*					
2021	Collin Morikawa	-15	265	2	Jordan Spieth	Royal St George's
2022	Cameron Smith	-20	268	1	Cameron Young	St Andrews

RECORDS

Most Victories

6: Harry Vardon, 1896, 1898, 1899, 1903, 1911, 1914
5: James Braid, 1901, 1905, 1906, 1908, 1910; JH Taylor, 1894, 1895, 1900, 1909, 1913; Peter Thomson, 1954, 1955, 1956, 1958, 1965; Tom Watson, 1975, 1977, 1980, 1982, 1983

Most Runner-Up or Joint Runner-Up Finishes

7: Jack Nicklaus, 1964, 1967, 1968, 1972, 1976, 1977, 1979
6: JH Taylor, 1896, 1904, 1905, 1906, 1907, 1914

Oldest Winners

Tom Morris Sr, 1867, 46 years 102 days
Roberto de Vicenzo, 1967, 44 years 92 days
Harry Vardon, 1914, 44 years 41 days
Tom Morris Sr, 1864, 43 years 92 days
Phil Mickelson, 2013, 43 years 35 days
Darren Clarke, 2011, 42 years 337 days
Ernie Els, 2012, 42 years 279 days

Youngest Winners

Tommy Morris Jr, 1868, 17 years 156 days
Tommy Morris Jr, 1869, 18 years 150 days
Tommy Morris Jr, 1870, 19 years 148 days
Willie Auchterlonie, 1893, 21 years 22 days
Tommy Morris Jr, 1872, 21 years 146 days
Seve Ballesteros, 1979, 22 years 103 days

Known Oldest and Youngest Competitors

74 years, 11 months, 24 days: Tom Morris Sr, 1896
74 years, 4 months, 9 days: Gene Sarazen, 1976
14 years, 4 months, 25 days: Tommy Morris Jr, 1865

Largest Margin of Victory

13 strokes, Tom Morris Sr, 1862
12 strokes, Tommy Morris Jr, 1870
11 strokes, Tommy Morris Jr, 1869
8 strokes, JH Taylor, 1900 and 1913; James Braid, 1908; Tiger Woods, 2000

Lowest Winning Total by a Champion

264: Henrik Stenson, Royal Troon, 2016 – 68, 65, 68, 63
265: Collin Morikawa, Royal St George's, 2021 – 67, 64, 68, 66
267: Greg Norman, Royal St George's, 1993 – 66, 68, 69, 64
268: Tom Watson, Turnberry, 1977 – 68, 70, 65, 65; Nick Price, Turnberry, 1994 – 69, 66, 67, 66; Jordan Spieth, Royal Birkdale, 2017 – 65, 69, 65, 69; Cameron Smith, St Andrews, 2022 – 67, 64, 73, 64

Lowest Total in Relation to Par Since 1963

20 under par: Henrik Stenson, 2016 (264); Cameron Smith, St Andrews, 2022 (268)
19 under par: Tiger Woods, St Andrews, 2000 (269)
18 under par: Nick Faldo, St Andrews, 1990 (270); Tiger Woods, Royal Liverpool, 2006 (270)

Lowest Total by a Runner-Up

267: Phil Mickelson, Royal Troon, 2016 – 63, 69, 70, 65; Jordan Spieth, Royal St George's, 2021 – 65, 67, 69, 66

Lowest Total by an Amateur

277: Jordan Niebrugge, St Andrews, 2015 – 67, 73, 67, 70

Lowest Individual Round

62: Branden Grace, third round, Royal Birkdale, 2017
63: Mark Hayes, second round, Turnberry, 1977; Isao Aoki, third round, Muirfield, 1980; Greg Norman, second round, Turnberry, 1986; Paul Broadhurst, third round, St Andrews, 1990; Jodie Mudd, fourth round, Royal Birkdale, 1991; Nick Faldo, second round, Royal St George's, 1993; Payne Stewart, fourth round, Royal St George's, 1993; Rory McIlroy, first round, St Andrews, 2010; Phil Mickelson, first round, Royal Troon, 2016; Henrik Stenson, fourth round, Royal Troon, 2016; Haotong Li, fourth round, Royal Birkdale, 2017; Shane Lowry, third round, Royal Portrush, 2019

Lowest Individual Round by an Amateur

65: Tom Lewis, first round, Royal St George's, 2011; Matthias Schmid, second round, Royal St George's, 2021

Lowest First Round

63: Rory McIlroy, St Andrews, 2010; Phil Mickelson, Royal Troon, 2016

Lowest Second Round

63: Mark Hayes, Turnberry, 1977; Greg Norman, Turnberry, 1986; Nick Faldo, Royal St George's, 1993

Lowest Third Round

62: Branden Grace, Royal Birkdale, 2017

Lowest Fourth Round

63: Jodie Mudd, Royal Birkdale, 1991; Payne Stewart, Royal St George's, 1993; Henrik Stenson, Royal Troon, 2016; Haotong Li, Royal Birkdale, 2017

Lowest Score over the First 36 Holes

129: Louis Oosthuizen, Royal St George's, 2021 – 64, 65

Lowest Score over the Middle 36 Holes

130: Fuzzy Zoeller, Turnberry, 1994 – 66, 64; Shane Lowry, Royal Portrush, 2019 – 67, 63

Lowest Score over the Final 36 Holes

130: Tom Watson, Turnberry, 1977 – 65, 65; Ian Baker-Finch, Royal Birkdale, 1991 – 64, 66; Anders Forsbrand, Turnberry, 1994 – 66, 64; Marc Leishman, St Andrews, 2015 – 64, 66

Lowest Score over the First 54 Holes

197: Shane Lowry, Royal Portrush, 2019 – 67, 67, 63
198: Tom Lehman, Royal Lytham & St Annes, 1996 – 67, 67, 64; Louis Oosthuizen, Royal St George's, 2021 – 64, 65, 69

Lowest Score over the Final 54 Holes

196: Henrik Stenson, Royal Troon, 2016 – 65, 68, 63
198: Collin Morikawa, Royal St George's, 2021 – 64, 68, 66; Jon Rahm, Royal St George's, 2021 – 64, 68, 66

Lowest Score for Nine Holes

28: Denis Durnian, first nine, Royal Birkdale, 1983
29: Tom Haliburton, first nine, Royal Lytham & St Annes, 1963; Peter Thomson, first nine, Royal Lytham & St Annes, 1963; Tony Jacklin, first nine, St Andrews, 1970; Bill Longmuir, first nine, Royal Lytham & St Annes, 1979; David J Russell first nine, Royal Lytham & St Annes, 1988; Ian Baker-Finch, first nine, St Andrews, 1990; Paul Broadhurst, first nine, St Andrews, 1990; Ian Baker-Finch, first nine, Royal Birkdale, 1991; Paul McGinley, first nine, Royal Lytham & St Annes, 1996; Ernie Els, first nine, Muirfield, 2002; Sergio Garcia, first nine, Royal Liverpool, 2006; David Lingmerth, first nine, St Andrews, 2015; Matt Kuchar, first nine, Royal Birkdale, 2017; Branden Grace, first nine, Royal Birkdale, 2017; Ryan Fox, second nine, Royal Portrush, 2019

Most Successive Victories

4: Tommy Morris Jr, 1868-72 (No Championship in 1871)
3: Jamie Anderson, 1877-79; Bob Ferguson, 1880-82; Peter Thomson, 1954-56
2: Tom Morris Sr, 1861-62; JH Taylor, 1894-95; Harry Vardon, 1898-99; James Braid, 1905-06; Bobby Jones, 1926-27; Walter Hagen, 1928-29; Bobby Locke, 1949-50; Arnold Palmer, 1961-62; Lee Trevino, 1971-72; Tom Watson, 1982-83; Tiger Woods, 2005-06; Padraig Harrington, 2007-08

Amateurs Who Have Won The Open

3: Bobby Jones, Royal Lytham & St Annes, 1926; St Andrews, 1927; Royal Liverpool, 1930
2: Harold Hilton, Muirfield, 1892; Royal Liverpool, 1897
1: John Ball Jr, Prestwick, 1890

Champions Who Won on Debut

Willie Park Sr, Prestwick, 1860; Tom Kidd, St Andrews, 1873; Mungo Park, Musselburgh, 1874; Jock Hutchison, St Andrews, 1921; Denny Shute, St Andrews, 1933; Ben Hogan, Carnoustie, 1953; Tony Lema, St Andrews, 1964; Tom Watson, Carnoustie, 1975; Ben Curtis, Royal St George's, 2003; Collin Morikawa, Royal St George's, 2021

Attendance

Year	Total
1960	39,563
1961	21,708
1962	37,098
1963	24,585
1964	35,954
1965	32,927
1966	40,182
1967	29,880
1968	51,819
1969	46,001
1970	81,593
1971	70,076
1972	84,746
1973	78,810
1974	92,796
1975	85,258
1976	92,021
1977	87,615
1978	125,271
1979	134,501
1980	131,610
1981	111,987
1982	133,299
1983	142,892
1984	193,126
1985	141,619
1986	134,261
1987	139,189
1988	191,334
1989	160,639
1990	208,680
1991	189,435
1992	146,427
1993	141,000
1994	128,000
1995	180,000
1996	170,000
1997	176,000
1998	195,100
1999	157,000
2000	239,000
2001	178,000
2002	161,500
2003	183,000
2004	176,000
2005	223,000
2006	230,000
2007	154,000
2008	201,500
2009	123,000
2010	201,000
2011	180,100
2012	181,300
2013	142,036
2014	202,917
2015	237,024
2016	173,134
2017	235,000
2018	172,000
2019	237,750
2021	152,330
2022	290,000

Greatest Interval Between First and Last Victory

19 years: JH Taylor, 1894-1913
18 years: Harry Vardon, 1896-1914
15 years: Willie Park Sr, 1860-75; Gary Player, 1959-74
14 years: Henry Cotton, 1934-48

Greatest Interval Between Victories

11 years: Henry Cotton, 1937-48 *(No Championship 1940-45)*
10 years: Ernie Els, 2002-12
9 years: Willie Park Sr, 1866-75; Bob Martin, 1876-85; JH Taylor, 1900-09; Gary Player, 1959-68

Champions Who Have Won in Three Separate Decades

Harry Vardon, 1896, 1898 & 1899/1903/1911 & 1914
JH Taylor, 1894 & 1895/1900 & 1909/1913
Gary Player, 1959/1968/1974

Competitors with the Most Top Five Finishes

16: JH Taylor; Jack Nicklaus

Competitors Who Have Recorded the Most Rounds Under Par From 1963

59: Jack Nicklaus
54: Nick Faldo, Ernie Els

Competitors with the Most Finishes Under Par From 1963

15: Ernie Els
14: Jack Nicklaus; Nick Faldo
13: Tom Watson

Champions Who Have Led Outright After Every Round

72 hole Championships
Ted Ray, 1912; Bobby Jones, 1927; Gene Sarazen, 1932; Henry Cotton, 1934; Tom Weiskopf, 1973; Tiger Woods, 2005; Rory McIlroy, 2014
36 hole Championships
Willie Park Sr, 1860 and 1866; Tom Morris Sr, 1862 and 1864; Tommy Morris Jr, 1869 and 1870; Mungo Park, 1874; Jamie Anderson, 1879; Bob Ferguson, 1880, 1881, 1882; Willie Fernie, 1883; Jack Simpson, 1884; Hugh Kirkaldy, 1891

Largest Leads Since 1892

After 18 holes:
5 strokes: Sandy Herd, 1896
4 strokes: Harry Vardon, 1902; Jim Barnes, 1925; Christy O'Connor Jr, 1985
After 36 holes:
9 strokes: Henry Cotton, 1934
6 strokes: Abe Mitchell, 1920
After 54 holes:
10 strokes: Henry Cotton, 1934
7 strokes: Harry Vardon, 1903; Tony Lema, 1964
6 strokes: JH Taylor, 1900; James Braid, 1905; James Braid, 1908; Max Faulkner, 1951; Tom Lehman, 1996; Tiger Woods, 2000; Rory McIlroy, 2014

Champions Who Had Four Rounds, Each Better than the One Before

Jack White, Royal St George's, 1904 – 80, 75, 72, 69
James Braid, Muirfield, 1906 – 77, 76, 74, 73
Ben Hogan, Carnoustie, 1953 – 73, 71, 70, 68
Gary Player, Muirfield, 1959 – 75, 71, 70, 68

Same Number of Strokes in Each of the Four Rounds by a Champion

Denny Shute, St Andrews, 1933 – 73, 73, 73, 73 (excluding the play-off)

Best 18-Hole Recovery by a Champion

George Duncan, Deal, 1920. Duncan was 13 strokes behind the leader, Abe Mitchell, after 36 holes and level with him after 54.

Greatest Variation Between Rounds by a Champion

14 strokes: Henry Cotton, 1934, second round 65, fourth round 79
12 strokes: Henry Cotton, 1934, first round 67, fourth round 79
11 strokes: Jack White, 1904, first round 80, fourth round 69; Greg Norman, 1986, first round 74, second round 63; Greg Norman, 1986, second round 63, third round 74
10 strokes: Seve Ballesteros, 1979, second round 65, third round 75

Greatest Variation Between Two Successive Rounds by a Champion

11 strokes: Greg Norman, 1986, first round 74, second round 63; Greg Norman, 1986, second round 63, third round 74

Greatest Comeback by a Champion

After 18 holes
Harry Vardon, 1896, 11 strokes behind the leader
After 36 holes
George Duncan, 1920, 13 strokes behind the leader
After 54 holes
Paul Lawrie, 1999, 10 strokes behind the leader

Champions Who Had Four Rounds Under 70

Greg Norman, Royal St George's, 1993 – 66, 68, 69, 64; Nick Price, Turnberry, 1994 – 69, 66, 67, 66; Tiger Woods, St Andrews, 2000 – 67, 66, 67, 69; Henrik Stenson, Royal Troon, 2016 – 68, 65, 68, 63; Jordan Spieth, Royal Birkdale, 2017 – 65, 69, 65, 69; Collin Morikawa, Royal St George's, 2021 – 67, 64, 68, 66

Competitors Who Failed to Win The Open Despite Having Four Rounds Under 70

Ernie Els, Royal St George's, 1993 – 68, 69, 69, 68; Jesper Parnevik, Turnberry, 1994 – 68, 66, 68, 67; Ernie Els, Royal Troon, 2004 – 69, 69, 68, 68; Rickie Fowler, Royal Liverpool, 2014 – 69, 69, 68, 67; Jordan Spieth, Royal St George's, 2021 – 65, 67, 69, 66; Mackenzie Hughes, Royal St George's, 2021 – 66, 69, 68, 69

Lowest Final Round by a Champion

63: Henrik Stenson, Royal Troon, 2016
64: Greg Norman, Royal St George's, 1993; Cameron Smith, St Andrews, 2022
65: Tom Watson, Turnberry, 1977; Seve Ballesteros, Royal Lytham & St Annes, 1988; Justin Leonard, Royal Troon, 1997

Worst Round by a Champion Since 1939

78: Fred Daly, third round, Royal Liverpool,
77: Dick Burton, third round, St Andrews, 1939
76: Bobby Locke, second round, Royal St George's, 1949; Paul Lawrie, third round, Carnoustie, 1999

Champion with the Worst Finishing Round Since 1939

75: Sam Snead, St Andrews, 1946

Lowest Opening Round by a Champion

65: Louis Oosthuizen, St Andrews, 2010; Jordan Spieth, Royal Birkdale, 2017

Most Open Championship Appearances

46: Gary Player
43: Sandy Lyle
38: Sandy Herd, Jack Nicklaus, Tom Watson
37: Nick Faldo

Most Final Day Appearances Since 1892

32: Jack Nicklaus
31: Sandy Herd
30: JH Taylor
28: Ted Ray
27: Harry Vardon, James Braid, Nick Faldo
26: Peter Thomson, Gary Player, Tom Watson

Most Appearances by a Champion Before His First Victory

19: Darren Clarke, 2011; Phil Mickelson, 2013
15: Nick Price, 1994
14: Sandy Herd, 1902
13: Ted Ray, 1912; Jack White, 1904; Reg Whitcombe, 1938; Mark O'Meara, 1998
11: George Duncan, 1920; Nick Faldo, 1987; Ernie Els, 2002; Stewart Cink, 2009; Zach Johnson, 2015; Henrik Stenson, 2016

The Open Which Provided the Greatest Number of Rounds Under 70 Since 1946

169 rounds, Royal St George's, 2021

The Open with the Fewest Rounds Under 70 Since 1946

2 rounds, St Andrews, 1946; Royal Liverpool, 1947; Carnoustie, 1968

Statistically Most Difficult Hole Since 1982

St Andrews, 1984, Par-4 17th, 4.79

Longest Course in Open History

Carnoustie, 2007, 7,421 yards

Number of Times Each Course Has Hosted The Open

St Andrews, 30; Prestwick, 24; Muirfield, 16; Royal St George's, 15; Royal Liverpool, 12; Royal Lytham & St Annes, 11; Royal Birkdale, 10; Royal Troon, 9; Carnoustie, 8; Musselburgh, 6; Turnberry, 4; Royal Cinque Ports, 2; Royal Portrush, 2; Prince's, 1

Increases in Prize Money (£)

Year	Total	First Prize	Year	Total	First Prize	Year	Total	First Prize	Year	Total	First Prize
1860	nil	nil	1891	28.50	10	1969	30,000	4,250	1996	1,400,000	200,000
1863	10	nil	1892	110	35	1970	40,000	5,250	1997	1,600,000	250,000
1864	15	6	1893	100	30	1971	45,000	5,500	1998	1,800,000	300,000
1865	20	8	1900	125	50	1972	50,000	5,500	1999	2,000,000	350,000
1866	11	6	1910	135	50	1975	75,000	7,500	2000	2,750,000	500,000
1867	16	7	1920	225	75	1977	100,000	10,000	2001	3,300,000	600,000
1868	12	6	1927	275	75	1978	125,000	12,500	2002	3,800,000	700,000
1872	unknown	8	1930	400	100	1979	155,000	15,000	2003	3,900,000	700,000
1873	unknown	11	1931	500	100	1980	200,000	25,000	2004	4,000,000	720,000
1874	20	8	1946	1,000	150	1982	250,000	32,000	2007	4,200,000	750,000
1876	27	10	1949	1,500	300	1983	310,000	40,000	2010	4,800,000	850,000
1877	20	8	1951	1,700	300	1984	451,000	55,000	2011	5,000,000	900,000
1878	unknown	8	1953	2,500	500	1985	530,000	65,000	2013	5,250,000	945,000
1879	47	10	1954	3,500	750	1986	600,000	70,000	2014	5,400,000	975,000
1880	unknown	8	1955	3,750	1,000	1987	650,000	75,000	2015	6,300,000	1,150,000
1881	21	8	1958	4,850	1,000	1988	700,000	80,000	2016	6,500,000	1,175,000
1882	47.25	12	1959	5,000	1,000	1989	750,000	80,000	2017	$10,250,000	$1,845,000
1883	20	8	1960	7,000	1,250	1990	825,000	85,000	2018	$10,500,000	$1,890,000
1884	23	8	1961	8,500	1,400	1991	900,000	90,000	2019	$10,750,000	$1,935,000
1885	35.50	10	1963	8,500	1,500	1992	950,000	95,000	2021	$11,500,000	$2,070,000
1886	20	8	1965	10,000	1,750	1993	1,000,000	100,000	2022	$14,000,000	$2,500,000
1889	22	8	1966	15,000	2,100	1994	1,100,000	110,000			
1890	29.50	13	1968	20,000	3,000	1995	1,250,000	125,000			

PHOTOGRAPHY CREDITS

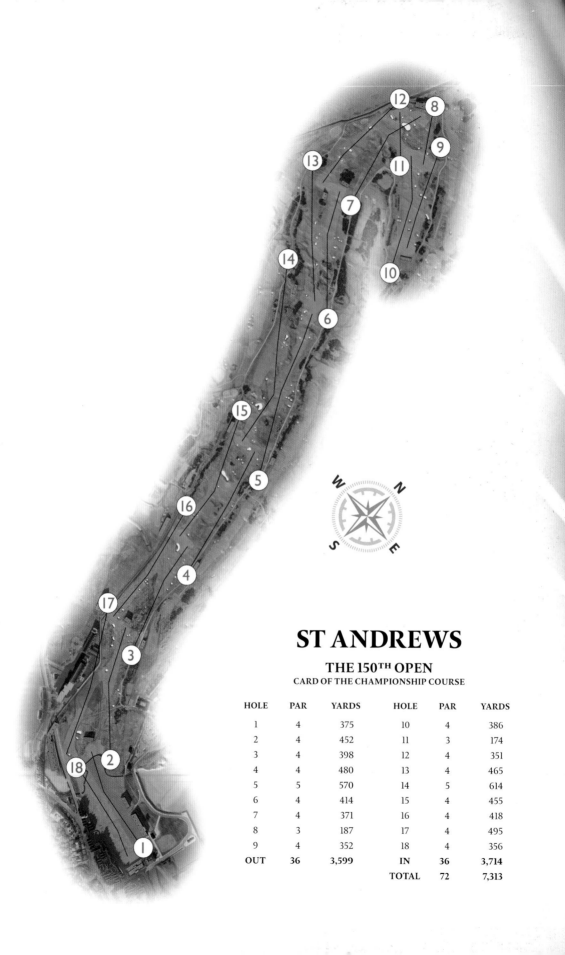

ST ANDREWS

THE 150TH OPEN
CARD OF THE CHAMPIONSHIP COURSE

HOLE	PAR	YARDS	HOLE	PAR	YARDS
1	4	375	10	4	386
2	4	452	11	3	174
3	4	398	12	4	351
4	4	480	13	4	465
5	5	570	14	5	614
6	4	414	15	4	455
7	4	371	16	4	418
8	3	187	17	4	495
9	4	352	18	4	356
OUT	36	3,599	IN	36	3,714
			TOTAL	72	7,313